INDIAN MUSLIM LABOUR

INDIAN MUSLIM LABOUR

AFZAL SHARIEFF

ANMOL PUBLICATIONS PVT. LTD.
NEW DELHI-110 002 (INDIA)

ANMOL PUBLICATIONS PVT. LTD.
4374/4B, Ansari Road, Daryaganj,
New Delhi-110 002

Indian Muslim Labour

First Edition 1998

ISBN 81-7488-922-1

PRINTED IN INDIA

Published by J.L. Kumar for Anmol Publications Pvt. Ltd., New Delhi-110 002, Typeset at Jain Computers, Delhi and Printed at Mehra Offset Press, Delhi.

CONTENTS

ACKNOWLEDGEMENTS

I wish to present my profound gratitude to Professor R. Ram Mohan Rao, who constantly and relentlessly kept my spirits alive to complete the present work. Professor Fatima Ali Khan was always keen to see the completion of my work, she constantly reminded me to finish my job at the earliest. I would like to express my gratitude to her. My colleagues, Vijaya Bhole, Kalpana Markanday, Simhadri helped me in the completion of my task. I extend my thanks to them.

My senior teacher, Professor K. Vithal Reddy always remained a pillar of inspiration. In his heart of hearts, he wanted that I should complete my work at the earliest. I am grateful to him.

I also extend my sincere gratitude to the Kuwaiti repatriated workers of Hyderabad, particularly my respondents and the Executive Committee Members of the Indo-Kuwait Friendship (IKF). They always welcomed my presence and responded to all my queries patiently and honestly. I remained grateful for their cooperation.

Dr. Inayatur-Rahman, helped me in my research data collection. Dr. Ramkishan Rao helped me in bringing the computerised graphs. I shall remain thankful to all these friends.

I shall be failing in my duty if I do not acknowledge my gratitude to a family (Mr. Shakeel Ahmad, Assistant Registrar, Hamdard University, New Delhi, Dr. S. Mehartaj Begum, Lecturer in Human

Rights, Department of Political Science, Jamia Millia Islamia, New Delhi and their two kids Master Faran Ahmad and Master Faizan Ahmad) for their support and encouragement for the publication of this book.

Finally, I am grateful to all those who directly or indirectly helped me in the completion of the present work in and outside the Department.

AFZAL SHARIEFF

1
INTRODUCTION

Man is a mobile creature, capable of enquiring, susceptible to suggestion, and endowed with imagination and initiative. This explains why, having conceived the notion that his wants might be satisfied elsewhere, he may decide, not merely on going where, but also on the means by which his project can be achieved (Garner, 1966). Many of the world's most acute social problems are associated with migration. Bogue (1969) has observed that "if the problem of Fertility was not so critical today, it is almost certain that the plight of the migrant, especially in the third world, would be listed as priority for research and action". The major cause of the migration is that it gets a big social change in the society. Migration is an independent as well as a dependent factor. Of the three components of population change, migration is the most complex and difficult phenomena and most important factor in differential population trends to analyse. The difference in demographical, socio-economic conditions of the people, is well attributed to the factor of migration.

Migration at the outset is a two way process: it is a response to socio-economic change and a catalyst to change for areas gaining and losing migrants. The latter always contributes and initiates new ideas, values and skills at the new place of residence. Birth, Death, and migration rates are the three components of population change. Migration has widespread consequences for the individual migrant, for the community of origin and destination, and also for the society within which the movement takes place.

The importance and the understanding of the migration of the human organizations is extensively covered by various authors—Pryor

(1971), Shaw (1975), Sharma (1978), Cleason and Egero (1972).They summarized that a knowledge of population movement is a consequence of both cause and effect of social processes and it remains as fundamental to a complete understanding of social change, economic development and political organization.

According to Simmie (1972) there are at least four reasons as to why an understanding of human migration is important:

1. Of all the uncertainties which plague population forecasting for local areas the greatest relate to migration as a source of change.
2. Migration itself may influence many other forms of spatial behaviour. The place of residence chosen largely determines the set of locations available for daily activities and whether this movement be over short or long distances it forms the basis of how people sift and sort themselves residentially in space.
3. An understanding of why families change their place of residence is fundamental for those involved with Urban development. They will be in a better position with such knowledge not only to guide private and public housing schemes but also to reduce the socio-economic problems caused by haphazard residential developments (Claerk and Moore) 1980.
4. How and why employers and employees move from one region to another is of crucial importance in any explanation of differential economic development. With such knowledge economists and regional Analysts are better able to channel development into desired localities and regions.

Most of the social sciences directly or indirectly do study migration. Each of the discipline has its own distinctive perception. Economists study migration in terms of jobs and other economic opportunities (Shaw 1975, Todaro 1976). Demographers are mainly concerned with the role of migration on the population growth and change, particularly in terms of population projections (Bogue 1969). The migrants character is studied by the socialists Mangalam (1968), Jackson (1969), Jansen (1970). Anthropologists are concerned with the problems faced by migrant groups within a host community Spencer (1970), Brandes (1975). The geographers perceive the problem with emphasis on the spatial pattern and locational decisions involved with migration Lewis (1974), Kosinsky, Protherto (1975).

Migration studiesowe much to interdisciplinary efforts, hence to isolate and segregate is a difficult task. Another problem is the weak theoretical base Willis (1974). The dearth of data and its consequent analysis restricts to classify various migration types. However, migration basically involves spatial and temporal dimensions, hence it is deemed a basically geographical and fundamentally a spatial process. It has three distinctive themes viz. the spatial pattern, the locational decisions and impact of migration at both the ends.

Approaches to the Study of Migration

Geographers, basically have adopted a behavioural approach to analyse the studies on migration. This involves disaggregation of population into groups and individuals of movers and stayers, Decision-making, perception, information, economic potential and the process of procuring the visa and the passport. However this approach is criticized for all decisions made are in a highly constrained situation Ward (1980). This approach basically provides more for individual choicc than groups. Thc second approach is to study the structure of the society, the role played by the Government, Agencies, Organizations and Institutions who determine and direct individuals migratory potential in terms of employment, wages and housing opportunities.The traditional approach of the geographer to study migration involved use of aggregate ideas and concepts. It was attached to the available theories, so any pattern of migration is considered to be the result of differences in opportunities between areas.

Approach to the Present Study

The present study is a retrospective and prospective approach. The Hyderabadi workers before going to Kuwait had a certain type of standard of living, employment, housing conditions and were subjected to certain cultural atmosphere. The retrospective socio-economic and Housing conditions is elicited from the repatriated Hyderabadi workers from Kuwait. Efforts are made to substantiate and study the existing and future living standards as a prospective approach. The rehabilitation issues are considered effectively to substantiate the future prospects based on the present living standards and assets.

Concepts of Migration

Migration is a situation of permanent or semi-permanent change of residence of an individual or a group of people. In terms of demographic balancing equation it is (Lewis, 1982):

Pt = Po + B - D + IM - Om

where,

Pt = Population at the close of interval

Po = Population at the beginning of the interval

B = Number of births in the interval

D = Number of deaths in the interval

Im = Number of Immigrants in the interval

Om = Number of out-migrants in the interval.

The equation envisages a population system in which the population at time Pt is equal to the population at the earlier time, Po, plus or minus change due to births (fertility), deaths (mortality) and migration in the interval between Pt and Po. Clearly a migrant is a person entering (in-migration) or leaving (out migration) a place by means other than their births or deaths and the total gross increments caused by such entrants or departure constitute migration. The difference between births and deaths is often referred to as natural change and the difference between in migration and out-migration is referred to as net migration.

In addition to the population change, migration in geographical perspective also involves certain additional dimensions for instance "for the change of residence of an individual from one parish or commune to another Hagerstrand (1957). The interval between the date of arrival and the date of departure; Weinberg (1961) stated that "migration is the changing of the place of abode permanently or, when temporarily, for an appreciable duration". It is used symbolically in the transition from one surrounding to another in the course of human life. Migration also involves a socio-cultural change in a new social set-up. This involves a weaking of socio-cultural ties with place of origin and adaptation to newer social ethos in the place of destination. Hence a "physical transition of an individual or a group from one society to another also involves abandoning of one social setting and entering another and different one" Eisenstandt (1953).

Mangalam (1968) stated that migration is a relatively permanent moving away of a collectively, called migrants, from one geographical location to another, preceded by decision making on the part of the migrants on the basis of a hierarchically ordered set of values or valued ends and resulting in changes in the interactional system of the migrants.

Zelinsky (1971) urged "Genuine migration obviously means the perceptible and simultaneous shifts in both spatial and social locus, so that the student can relistically measure one kind of movement and he ignores the other - ideally, we should observe shifts in both varieties of space in tandem but given the dearth of techniques and data for handling purely social movement, we are forced to solely rely on territorial movements as a clumsy surrogate for total mobility".

The concept to the present study of migration is associated with a semi-permanent residence change. Geographically it is a territorial movement and it is a temporary movement for an appreciable duration of time. It is a transitory situation from one surrounding to another in the course of human life. It is also a socio-cultural and economic change in a given new set-up. The Migrant despite placed in a new physical and social interaction is still conservative, and innovator and that he had never deserted his traditional culture, even after a long duration of stay abroad. His economic condition has substantially elevated and consequent to this the standard of living has clandestingly changed. The impact of which is distinctly visible in housing, Assets, transport, children's education and other activities of life. The overall social and urban society has witnessed physical and human transformation in the place of origin. Streams of migrants who left for better prospects, consolidated their stay to a substantial time and shifted to their original occupations. A drastic change is associated contrary to their past living conditions.

Mobility

Mobility is a general term which includes all types of territorial movements, including migrations. A distinction is necessary between spatial or geographical mobility and social mobility, a term used to cover changes in socio-economic status. Not all forms of social mobility may be regarded as migration. The latter usually implies a permanent or semi-permanent change of residence and therefore excludes, for example commuters, holiday makers, and students moving termly between family house and college. These forms of mobility are often designated as "circulation" which cover a great variety of movements, usually short-term, repetitive or cyclical in character, but all having in common the lack of any declared intention of a permanent or long lasting change in residence, Zelinsky (1971). The latter further developed the idea of the "mobility transition" related to the general model of the "demographic transition," in which he hypothesizes a relation between different types of movements and general process of urbanisation, industrialization and modernisation in space and time.

Migration Scale

Scale provides an essential criterion for classification, so migration may be international, inter-regional, inter-urban rural-urban or intra-urban. Other criteria include time, (temporary/permanent) distance, (long/short) decision-making (voluntary/forced) numbers involved, (individual/mass) social organization of migrants, (family/class/individuals) political organization, (sponsored/free) causes, (economic/social) and aims, (conservative/innovative). The present study is of the international migration basically, urban to urban, temporarily long distance movement. The decision is voluntary and it involved individual and mass (groups) moving. The social organization includes, individuals, family and essentially one community of people i.e. muslims. The migrants are sponsored and also contract labour. The major cause of migration is economic and their aim is both conservative and innovative.

Migration Theories/Laws

There is, no comprehensive theory of migration, although, attempts have been made to integrate migration into economic and social theory, spatial analysis and behavioural theory. In the late nineteenth century, E.G. Ravenstein formulated what he called "Laws of Migration" on which much subsequent work has been based Grigg (1977). These were:

(a) the majority of migrants go only a short distance;

(b) migration proceeds step by step;

(c) migrants going long distances generally go by preference to one of the great centres of commerce of industry;

(d) each current of migration produces a compensating counter current;

(e) the natives of towns are less migratory than those of rural areas;

(f) females are more migratory than males within their country of birth, but males more frequently venture beyond;

(g) most migrants are adults - families rarely migrate out of their country of birth;

(h) large towns grow more by migration than by natural increase;

(i) migration increases in volume as industries and commerce develop and transport improves;

(j) the major direction of migration is from the agricultural areas to the centres of industry and commerce;

(k) the major causes of migration are economic;

these 'laws' have been modified by subsequent research rather than fundamentally disproved.

The present study does not have much of theory or that no new laws are established. It is in concurrance with Ravenstein's Laws viz "migrants going long distance generally go by preference, most of them are adults, families rarely migrate. The major causes of migration are economic. Their arrival in the host country has given importance of increase in population growth more by virtue of migration than by natural increase. The industrial, commercial and transport development of the pulling countries has increased the volume of migration to the so called Gulf Countries.

Type of Migrants

The definition of migrant excludes persons who cross a frontier into a foreign country to complete their education there, or for tourism, pilgrimage or nomadism.

Three main types of migrants:

Refugees, that is persons who feel their countries of residence owing to racial or religious persecutions on the ground of nationality or political opinion. It is generally agreed that the term refugees should be reserved for those mainly political catagories and that persons who leave their countries of residence for economic reasons, in particular poverty, are omitted.

Migrants who leave their countries of legal residence voluntarily and hence obtained legal authorization for entry and stay from the authorities of the recipient country. Some of these persons are granted all the economic rights enjoyed by nationals and, more rarely, the civil rights as well (right of vote). But others are subject to restrictions usually connected with the exercise of an economic activity. Some are granted authorization for a long-term stay, which sometimes enable them subsequently to acquire permanent residence or citizenship. Others, however, are admitted for a limited time, and are obliged to leave the country when their work is completed.

Illegal immigrants, who have not obtained permission to stay and thus escape, all statistical reckoning.

The use of place of birth is a good indicator of international migration. India has second largest number of persons born abroad, with almost 8 million, which is only 1-2 per cent of the Indian population.

The Gulf Countries

The countries of the Persian gulf namely, Bahrain, Kuwait, Saudi Arabia and the United Arab Emirates, have fairly high proportion of persons born abroad, and who were taken in mainly during the 1970s. In those countries, many immigrants had a limited residence permit in connection with the so called "keys in hands" projects. They came from North America, India, Republic of Korea, Pakistan, and Phillippines. In recent years, the recepient countries of this region have tended to adopt measures to regulate immigration and manpower recruitment more strictly and to ensure rotation of this man power.

In Kuwait, the foreign population nearly doubled between 1975-1985. In 1975 about 80 per cent of all the foreigners in Kuwait originated from other Arab countries, by 1985 only 63 per cent did so. The remainder came mostly from other Asian countries. Indeed, the late 1970s and early 1980s witnessed an important upsurge in the outflow of the migrant workers from countries in southern and S.E. Asia. Statistics on the number of persons granted temporary permission to work on contractual agreements show that by 1985, nearly one million persons were leaving their countries annually to work abroad in oil rich countries of W. Asia during 1975-79, four countries accounted for 87 per cent of annual number of migrant workers from India, Pakistan, Phillippines and Republic of Korea, Each contributing an equal number of emigrants. By 1980's Phillippines alone contributed to 45% and that of the share of other three countries remained to 30 per cent henceforth it kept on declining. India, by late 1970s had about 96 per cent of all migrant workers registered with the authorities of their decision to migrate to the S.W. Asian countries.

Gulf-Migration

"Employment of Indians in the south-west Asians countries and its impact on their socio-economic conditions - A case study of Kuwaiti Repatriates in Hyderabad." The title of the study in itself emphasizes the problem for rcscarch. The temporary labour exodus to the South-West Asian countries largely initiated from 1970. The Gasterbeitor (German term for temporary immigrant labour) from Hyderabad irrespective of the name or country of destination was willing to emigrate any where in the Gulf countries. The cycle of poverty, (inherited from the parents) the low literacy attainment, the unemployment sidearm, the large and heavy liabilities of the family burden evolved a cynical feeling to migrate from one cultural hearth to another.

The remnant army people of the erstwhile Nizam of Hyderabad who were brought from Yemen of Arabia and who were stranded in after the accession of the erstwhile Hyderabad into the Indian Republic faced dire socio-economic and cultural traits. At the beginning, for a decade 1950-1960, they struggled to make livelihood in the city. However, with their cultural contacts of their native homeland of Arabia recalled them. The cultural ties of these arabs made deep roots into their minds and marriages with non-Arabs forced them to migrate along with their wives and children from 1960 onwards to their ancestral homelonal. This initiated a small stream of these people moving back from Hyderabad to Arab Gulf.

The Chain and circulatory migration initiated fundamentally by the native Arabs of Hyderabad who provided a stronger base for the other kith and kin. Thus the chain continued from individuals to masses to emigrate, particularly to Saudi Arabia, U.A.E. and Kuwait.

Origin of the Immigrants Labour Force in Kuwait

The immigrant labour force in Kuwait comprised of a variety of nationalities, ethnic groups, culture and of different professional and educational standards. Kuwait prior to August 1990 had 68 different nationalities covering over 50 per cent of the total manpower in almost every sector of the economy. According to the 1980 Kuwaiti census, Arab nationals constituted 72.5 per cent, Asians 25 per cent and the rest were Europeans, Africans and Americans.

A detailed account of the immigrant manpower in Kuwait is published in the year 1975 by the Government of Kuwait. It showed 70 per cent Arabs viz Palestinians/Jordanians (22 per cent) Egyptians (13 per cent) and Iraqis (8.5 per cent). The 30 per cent Non-Arab constituted Iranians (13.7 per cent) Indians (10 per cent) Pakistanis and Others (5.2 per cent).

Kuwait has a free market, with giant development projects, particularly service oriented provided an better opportunity for the Hyderabadi Indians. It is found that above 50 per cent of the Hyderabadis joined as Transport Drivers, either in Government or semi-Government or private sectors, the second highest majority constituted of technical/skilled labour, then followed the service oriented/ministerial personnel. However, a very few Hyderabadis are conspicuous in the professional categories in Kuwait.

Manufacturing industry, construction and building and services comprised of 75.8 per cent of the total immigrant labour force in Kuwait. "Shuwaith" and "Ray" areas largely constituted of manufacturing Industry construction, while the service sector was concentrated in the Kuwait city.

Indians in Kuwait

The geographical distribution of Indians resembles that of the Iranians. Their concentration was in Kuwait town, Salmiya and Hawalli was respectively 39.3, 13.7 and 6.4 per cent of their total numbers.

In Kuwait Town where they make up 16.1 per cent of the total populations, they are basically employed as house maids and servants, Al-moosa (1985). On housing the Indians at an average paid KD 128.5 rent per month. The number of house-hold individuals was 3.9 for the Indians. Al-moosa (1985) estimated from his survey that prior to migration the Indians have been engaged mainly in three occupations in their home country: 38.7 per cent have been professional and technical workers, 27.0 per cent clerks and 21.0 per cent production and transportation workers.

Moosa, further emphasized that in Kuwait the Pakistanis and Indian immigrants are reluctant to join service work due Arabic language and social barriers. These two nationalities are concentrated on professional and technical works, as laborers, and in transportation jobs due to their work experience and ability to speak English language. They consequently after a longer duration of stay learn Arabic working language and enter other services depending upon the availability. Besides, knowledge of Arabic creates more confidence and makes way to procure multiple occupations. Jobs in sales sector calls for a preferably better Arabic.

Further, the Indians in Kuwait predominate in medical, laboratory, nursing, electronic, and secretarial jobs. They are found in jobs where the English language is used, especially in companies and corporations which deal with foreign sources. It is further observed that there is no significant change in their occupational structure regarding Kuwait and their country of origin. Al-moosa (1985)

The Objectives of the Study

1. To evaluate the retrospective and prospective socio-economic conditions of the house-holds of the Hyderabadi workers repatriated from Kuwait.

2. Selected socio-economic indicators viz., duration of stay, Age-sex composition, religion, educational standard, employment, income, expenditure, remittances and savings of the repartriated workers are to be assessed in Hyderabadi and in Kuwait.

3. To study the occupational change, the residential mobility within the city and its impact on their rehabilitation, problems and prospects of future living conditions.

Hypotheses of the Study

1. The Employment prospects of the Hyderabadi workers to Kuwait since 1970s resulted in drastic improvement in their socio-economic conditions, standards of living, better housing, purchase power of luxurious assets.
2. Remittances received were mostly spent in economically unproductive non-capital sectors like excessive marriage expenditure, purchase of plots and jewellery, electronic and luxurious goods, cars etc.
3. Occupational shift with resultant negative repurcussions are observed amongst the migrated workers to Kuwait and on return to Hyderabad.
4. The morphological structure of the Hyderabad city has drastically transformed. Rapid urbanisation, excessive commercial activity and physical expansion combined with cultural transformation became evident.
5. Emergence of new housing colonies in the city suburbs, filling up of vacant lands within the city, purchase of numerous plots in outskirts the city and leaving with no construction except for speculating high returns is conspicuous.
6. The repercussions of the migration is distinctly evident in all sectors of the city economy. The high purchase power of the latter restricted the local non-migrated citizens with limited options thereby making life dearer and competitive.

Study Area

The universe of the study area is confined to twenty three wards of the Hyderabad city. The city wards, viz., ward numbers twenty, twenty-one, twenty-two and twenty-three are unique, for, since four hundred years these wards and area (about 2.5 sq. kilometers) remained constant and was bounded by a wall all over. It is also called the walled city of Hyderabad. The famous monument Charminar is located in the central place of these four wards. Majority of the sample survey respondents have emerged from this area. In addition to this the south and south-eastern corners of the city, where a large number of muslim community is concentrated also appeared in the survey. There were also some respondents almost from each of the 23 wards.

The methodology adopted to study the present problem was by obtaining the detailed information through secondary sources as well as through a structured questionnaire consisting both open and closed ended questions. The questions were related to their before migration, during their stay in Kuwait and finally their returned condition and standard of living was elicited.

The format of the schedule included questions relating to socio-economic conditions, housing, assets, indebtedness, remittance sent from abroad, expenditure and income pattern, savings, purchase of real estate, plots and so on. The so-collected information was fed into the computer to draw quick results. After obtaining various tables from the raw data, graphs and maps drawn using suitable cartographic techniques and was subjected to analysis and interpretation.

The present study is inter-disciplinary, however major emphasis on laid upon the socio-economic and housing constraints. It is an attempt to understand major intention of the repatriates rehabilitation problems. There is no detailed study made on the Hyderabadi migrants to the south-west Asian countries in general and that to Kuwait in particular. Hence, the importance of the study need not be elaborated.

In order to enrich and substantiate additional subject information, the government and thc voluntary agencies spread all over the city were visited. These included in addition to the Kuwait's repatriates Association KRA, NISEF (Non-Resident Indian Socio-cconomic Foundation), IRJAA (Indian Resettlement Joint Advisory Association), ANRICH (Andhra Pradesh State Non-Resident Indians Investment Corporation Limited), CI (Commissioner of Industries).

After the Iraq's Invasion on Kuwait almost all the immigrants have returned back to their home countries. The Hyderabadi workers repatriated from Kuwait have formed themselves into "Kuwaitis Repatriate Association" (KRA). The aim of this association was to register the workers into a one group and request the central and state governments and also the Kuwaiti embassy, the United Nations about their problems. Their identity of stayed in Kuwait is produced, by means of identity cards, passports and other documents. They have appealed to the state government to issue the Gas Cylinders, admission into schools for their children and civil supplies ration card which is readily accepted.

The office of the Kuwaiti Repatriates Association KRA maintained a record of Presidential address in Kuwait and Hyderabad, Employment lost, last salary drawn, in Kuwait amount left over with the employer, in the banks, during their stay in Kuwait.

The Registrar of the registered candidates was utilized to stratification of all these members was made, based on from their occupations viz professionals, Technicians, service workers and Drivers. Following a thumb rule a 10 per cent sample of each of the categories is drawn, using the random table, the required number of respondents were subjected to detailed analysis. This amounted to 44 professionals, 60 each of the three other categories, amounting to 224 total respondents.

Chapter Scheme

The chapter scheme is designed to study, analyse and interpret the problems of the Kuwaiti repatriates of the Hyderabadi workers. Introductory and explorative issues are detailed in the first chapter. Extensive review of literature on the Kuwait and other related works is summarized. The methodology, data collection, hypothesis, objectives the sampling design and carleographic techniques obtained are presented.

The second chapter iks devoted to study of the over view of the Indians in the south-west Asian countries. The Analysis made by the various authors of different third world countries like Pakistan, Bangladesh, Philippines and Korean labour force emigration to various south-west Asian countries and its repercussions on their own country. The impact of foreign remittances on their country economy is also explored, particular emphasis laid on the immigrant labour in Kuwait.

The third chapter is concentrated on the study of social constraints associated with the Hyderabadi repatriated workers from Kuwait. Analysis of these workers during their stay in Kuwait with regards to their length of stay, educational backgrounds age, sex, marital status and religion.

The fourth chapter presents on analysis of the economic aspects of problems and constrains of the repratriates. Essentially the employment structure, the income and expenditure pattern the assets, the remittances sent its utilization is explained.

The fifth chapter highlights the housing problems, before and after migration to Kuwait. The condition of the housing, the investments on the plots purchased amount spent on house renovation owned and rented housing, number of rooms per person both at Kuwait and Hyderabad is presented. The residential mobility within the Hyderabad city of the repatriates after and before migration is also drawn.

The sixth chapter is the summary and conclusion of the thesis. This chapter attempts to summarize the various issues related to the migrants of the Hyderabad city to Kuwait. The economic growth, the social changes, the change in the standard of living and other issues relational to housing and rehabilitation are presented. An over view of the Gulf War impact on the Kuwait economy is briefly assessed. An overall picture of cultural change is also presented in the light of the information and analysis obtained.

Review of Literature

The review of literature is mostly drawn from the Arab scholars of the middle east. A limited work is found by the Indians. However, wherever their contributions are found, that has been accommodated. The review is drawn in addition to the Books, Journals and Ph.D dissertations and other various articles.

S.S. Kurup (1984) dealt with the plight of the Indian workers in the Gulf countries. He observed that the Indians, Pakistanis, Bangladeshis and Srilankans have been vying with each other for jobs in these countries. Countries such as Republic of Korea and Philippines also supply labour to Gulf, but these latter countries regulate wages and look after the well being of their citizens in the Gulf, monitor their living standards and other problems, whereas there are no such attempts with the governments of the former countries is the important observation presented by Karup.

Further, the Indians workers are totally under the mercy of their recruiting agent and the employer. Their living conditions are from bad to worse, they are frequently paid lower wages. The bulk of migrants are from Kerala in the age group of 25-30 years. Majority of them are males both bachelors and married. The scope for the female employment is limited. The dearth of accommodation is the main cause of taking their families with them.

Kurup emphasized the need for in-depth studies on the conditions of the migrants, their composition and the rate of return migration. The value at migration may increase upto 1995. In the year 1979, 1,72,000 people emigrated and in the subsequent years the figure was never below 2,36,000.

Kurup felt that there are studies of the Indians in the western countries, but a very little or negligible work is done on these minority populace to the Gulf. Neither the researchers nor the government has bothered to work into their welfare conditions. Though the government gains a great deal of foreign exchange from their remittances it has been totally callous about their conditions of existence. The government has its eye only on their remittances and plans of investment.

Partha S. Ghosh (1990) in his article on "our Gulf policy: some Nagging doubts", criticised the Indian policy on Afghan issue. During the Soviet intervention into Afghanistan, it is of direct relevance to our country. Further Ghosh criticised the Indian Policy with the Iraqi invasion of Kuwait and its subsequent annexation, the Indian response for its citizens standard in Kuwait and Jordan. He questioned, "India, one of the leaders of the Non-Aligned movement and which claims to be the champion of the world peace should rest content with that everyday one plane or two lift the stranded Indians are brought home."

Ghosh also pointed out Indians inability to register at least a word of protest on the Gulf warm and for its decision to close its embassy. In general, the neutral diplomacy of India on Iran-Iraq war and Kuwait's invasion is regretted.

Ghosh also observed the failure of the claims made by the Oil and Natural Gas Commission to fulfil its fuel needs. The large amounts of oil imports from the south-west Asian countries particularly Saudi Arabia Kuwait and U.A.E. The rise in prices of oil due to the war are the other economic jolts felt by the Indian Government. However, the country decided to stay quiet over such hardships and remained a mute spectator all over the process.

Prakash (1983) in his article on the impact of foreign remittances - A case study of Chavakkad village in Kerala, surveyed about 95 households in the Chavakkad village of Tiruchur district in the Kerala State. He discussed the issues related to those working abroad, money sent home and its impact on their income, consumption savings and investments pattern.

Prakash concluded that from each house-hold one to three persons had gone abroad, and the other unemployed are/were trying to go overseas. Before, their migration, those people were self employed, beedi workers, tailors, hotel workers, drivers and engaged in small scale business.

Due to severe unemployment, low income and education, forced the youth to flee in search of jobs to Bomaby and from there they ventured go overseas. The approximate expenditure on visa ranged between Rs. 2500 to 10,000. These movements have started from 1950s, but since 1974 it was the largest. These personnel accepted whatever job was available to them in the south west Asian countries of Arabia.

Each person residing in the Gulf sent approximately to Rs. 250 to 1000. Majority of the houses were in possession of radios, tape recorder and even cars. A substantial amount was invested on housing, this resulted in high land prices. One-third of the village witnessed new houses. The huge housing activity also resulted in steep price rise of the housing construction material.

Leela Gulati (1983) in her article on "male migrants to middle east and its impact on the family" - some evidence from kerala had presented her paper in two parts. The first part was a general trend and peoples movement to middle east from India and Kerala is depicted. Part two is confined to the impact as the family due to dominantly male members being migrated.

Leela, estimated about 150,000 Indian workers to middle east and 800,000 in 1975 and 1982 respectively. She also estimated as much as 20 per cent of the workers in the middle east are Indians.Her estimates of Kerala migrants to middle east was 135,000 in 1977 and 208,000 by the beginning of 1980. And it was 300,000 in 1983.

Leela concluded that the migration from Kerala State to middle east is substantial, majority of them are males hailing from certain regions and religion of the state. She also observed the migrants were young with low skills. The remittances sent by these migrants consequently and substantially improved their standards of living and housing.

The impact on the family, particularly, the women folk increased in their sex ratio, besides shouldering family responsibilities as Heads of the House-holds had a difficult time to maintain and manage finance, social values, and psychological stress and strain. The impact is also felt on the age at marriage, fertility of the women particularly, the young brides left over with the in-laws and their husbands staying away for long years. Finally, she observed that, when men return home, and settle down, the damage to intra-family relationship may well be beyond repair.

Monolo Abella, (1984) wrote an article on "Labour migration from South and South East Asia: some policy issues". The article was to analyse the growth and development of the sending countries impact on the country's economy, trade, employment. He quoted on India:

"The impact of overseas migration on the labour market appeals to have hardly been felt in India; even in such major states of emigration as Kerala, Karnataka, Maharashtra or Gujarat. In Kerala official sources reported that at least 300,000 Keralities lived abroad in 1979, largely in the Gulf countries. At the same time 1.2 million job seekers were registered with the employment exchanges in Kerala; half of these were educated, including 54,000 university graduates and 8,500 post graduates".

Rizwanul Islam (1980), observed on the impact of the recession on the developing countries of Asia, that without exception all the countries from South & South East Asia had suffered a deterioration on their barter terms of trade during the period from 1979 to 1982. He observed that in the absence of the overseas remittances, the balance of payment would have suffered a set-back.

Gulati and Mody (1983) on their paper on remittances of Indian migrants to the middle east; as assessment with special reference to migrants from Kerala calculated the remittance during 1978 were 1,310 million U.S. Dollars. It was 2554 million U.S. Dollars. Abella observed that these remittances became extremely useful for the balance of payments.

Abella, observed that the countries of South and South East Asia had a maximum of private licensed recruiting agents. It ranged between 28 per cent in Bangladesh to 95 per cent in Thailand. It is observed that India in the year 1980 had between 800 - 900 licensed private recruiters and ten government recruiting agents. The public sector recruiting agencies are in Kerala, Maharashtra, Tamil Nadu and Orissa.

The cash and surety bonds to obtain private license for recruitment in India ranged between 1,00,000 up for 100 workers to Rs. 5,00,000 for upto 1001 or more workers. (Deepak Nayyar 1989).

Abella observed, that the restrictions imposed under the immigration laws are waived by certain workers and socially objectionable occupations such as prostitution. They generally under declare their credentials and go as tourists. The frequent reports on "Imported prostitutes" in many countries of middle east are unwelcome reminders of the case with which prohibitions can be evaded. On the contract construction projects in middle east, India at the beginning of 1981 captured the total value of construction and civil engineering projects was almost 4400 million U.S. Dollars of which labour cost amounted to 16 to 20 per cent.

Osman H. Chowdhury (1986) in his paper on the "Labour migration to the middle east - An Asian perspective" reviewed the trend and pattern of Asian labour migration to the middle east. He viewed to look into the observed economic consequences for the sending countries in terms of remittances, balance of payments. He examined the cases of India, Pakistan, Bangladesh, Korea and Thailand.

Osman felt that Asian labour in South West Asian constituted 20 per cent in the year 1975 and increased to 30 per cent by 1980. Basically, Asians moved excessively into the Gulf from 1973 onwards. The Indians and the Pakistanis are the first to reach followed by other Asian nations. The Gulf Migration is divided into three phases. The first phase was inter-regional, where the poor Arabians moved into the oil rich zones followed by the Palestinians who were in exile. This phase ended by 1970, the second phase ended by 1973 constituted of Egyptians and Jordanians who filled the posts of teachers, administrators and professionals vacancy. The last phase was by the Asians, who have filled all the remaining gaps.

Three factors are identified by Osman on Asian to move into the Gulf viz. Religion; Non interference of the Asian in the regional politics of Arabia and great labour demand and better pay packages provided in these countries.

The middle eastern countries experienced a cosmopolitan culture and heterogeneous groups of immigrant nationals. This suppressed the domination of one or two countries or cultures over others. This enabled the host countries to carry over their policies of ruling peacefully. The host countries had "package deals" for the construction workers of the Asian countries. (Korea, Phillippines and Pakistan) these countries had their own labour to complete the projects and leave the host country.

Finally Osman concluded in his paper, that the Asian countries encouraged contract and private recruitment into middle east. The remittances received were largely helping in the balance of payments. Asians in addition to the semi-skilled and skilled labour also allowed certain professionals to immigrate, but only to have a short-term stay of these professionals obviously, the immigrant labour force families enjoyed a better socio-economic conditions. Housing and health, besides a comfortable savings and fixed assets into their credits.

Mathew and Nair attempted to study the "socio-economic characteristics of the emigrants and emigrants house-holds - A case study of two villages in Kerala". The article emphasized job opportunities abroad, socio-economic background of the emigrants, the subsequent income and its use, and the impact of the remittances on the states economy. They studied two villages of Kerala in the Trivandrum district.

The study area constituted of 50 per cent emigrants from "Perumathura" in Cheriyinkil panchayat and 40 per cent emigrates from Puthukurnchi in the Kadinamkulam Panchayat, both in the Trivandrum district.

The two villages represented different geographical conditions. Perumathura was a coastal village and Puthukurnchi is a dry village where not even a coconut tree is found. However, people in this village were well educated and economically sound than the other. The former migrants showed marked preference to construct new houses in the urban areas, hence always are in guest of land and prefer to settle in the state capital Tirmanantapuram. Both the villages had bank facilities. 90 per cent of the savings were generally drawn for consumption at every month end and only a small proportion over construction activities is spent. Residential land is at great demand, shortage of agricultural and construction labour is clearly felt.

Finally, it is concluded. Emigration is not confined to a homogenous socio-economic background. Emigrants had different educational and work experience in different fields. The demographic profile of the family size, age, sex ratio had a significant impact. However employment rates have not steadily fallen. The state witnessed a number of training centres of technical trades which is in demand in the middle east are emerging. Tremendous impact on the trade and business is evident and conspicuous in the states economic structure.

"The Immigrant labour force in Kuwait" (1985) by Al-Moosa, Abdul Rasool and Keith Mclain is an extensive exploratory study of the "Immigrant labour in Kuwait", their socio-economic conditions. The Geographical distribution of the immigrant workers, the housing conditions and the overall impact of the immigrated labour contribution on the Kuwait economy is dealt. The occupational shift, the educational standards, age, sex composition, income and employment characteristics particularly of the Egyptians, the Palestinians, the Jordanians of Arab origin and the Asian representatives from India, Pakistan, Bangladesh, Philippines, Korea, workers is presented in detail. This work can be considered as a pioneer study with detailed living conditions of the immigrant labour force in Kuwait after 1981 to the dawn of the Iraqi invasion on Kuwait.

Abdul Galal (1987) studied the urbanisation and the Labour Migration in the Arab countries of the Gulf and found the Gulf cities constitutes 50% of the expatriate labourers, the increased presser on housing, conflicts between migrants and indigenous population, ineptness in the production of indigenous workers socio-politico threat of the Arab culture, particularly from that of the Asian labour.

Mostafa (1988) explained, the community, the family and the individual migrant problem analysis, and highlights the extent to which the migration for work benefits the rural families in the third world, Broad consequences on the socio-economic conditions, the ubiquitous and bi-directional contribution of migration to economic growth, human welfare, dependency, inequality, the rise of new economic order other emerging forces, the rise of new economic order other emerging trends in the political economy of the middle east.

A-1 Moosa (1988) explored the soared employment consequences of urbanization in Kuwait, the rapid urbanisation and sprawling new institutions in Kuwait, the development of salarised employment as a significant aspect of socio-economic changes of Kuwait is observed. Changes in social norms, interpersonal relations, individual aspirations are highlighted. Traditional occupations which created interdependency between individuals and families were weakened or eliminated.

Khalidi (1991) presented an overview of the Persian Gulf crisis and analysed Iraqs reasons for invasion of Kuwait. Following an explanation of the Arab worlds support of Saddam Hussain, despite his aggression against Kuwait, potential scenarios for development of the crisis is discussed. It is argued that the US-Iraq conflict should be depersonalised that the trend towards maintenance of global security exhibited by the UNO active intervention should be strengthened and carried to other parts of the world. Suggestions for the peaceful resolution are proposed, including restoration of Kuwait's Sovereignty, Iraqs complete withdrawal from Kuwait, and return of stolen Kuwait assets & preservation of integrety on the part of Iraq. It is argued that the sanctions against Iraq should be maintained and tightened as an effective, though time limited, alternative to war.

Farah Tewfic E (1989) presented article on political culture and development in a Rentier state, the case of Kuwait is discussed, she proclaimed neither modernisation nor dependency theory explains how Kuwait has remained stable when other Gulf countries are in turmoil. The unique match between the political system and the political culture in Kuwait, a result of the management skills on the rulers, is believed responsible when Kuwait became fully independent in 1961, power was transferred to the Al-Sabah monarchy and its small closed family lines. Within this rentier state, to have the substantial portion of the revenue comes from foreign sources, the Al-Sabah monarch distribute the revenues to the political elite and the population at large. There are no income taxes, 66 per cent of the population is employed by the bureaucracy, which reinforces allegiance to the state. Opposition movements, like the nationalists and the Sunny Islamists, are controlled on two sides: favours & revenues are doled out while the Government maintains an active security force. Although comprising about 25 per cent of the population, Shia Islamists are outside of the mainstream of politics and muslim fundamentalism is warming. Recent periods of slack oil revenue's were offset by funds from investments, fending off any cutback in salaries and services and hence possible projects. This political system can be expected to survive for the socio-economic changes.

Al-Sahhaf Habeeb (1990) studied the "Human Resource Management in Kuwait". He argued, that there is no complete data analysed on Human Resource Management (HRM). The current practice in Kuwait HRM vary completely from routine to some attempts to adopt modern ideas. He observed that the Development of HRM field in Kuwait is not consistent with the available potential. Despite the existence of many constants and difficulties that prevent HRM from its potential development. The objective of his research was to define the existing HRM practices in different economic sectors within Kuwait. The concepts, features and practices of HRM are seen to be a consequence of socio-economic structure.

Ghabra Shafeeq (1991) is a Palestinian Professor of Political Science stranded in Kuwait from 2 August 1990 to October 1990 (the authors departure), described the invasion, attempts of resistance by the unprepared Kuwaiti Army- the realities created by the invasion-shortage of food, absence of news and lack of personal security. It is contented that the Iraqis consciously attempted to create an atmosphere of anarchy. Further accounts on Kuwait's formation, the Kuwaiti society and the tensions created between Palestinians and Kuwait's is described in his paper.

Oomen (1989) observed on brain drain and the migration of talented Indians exposed three basic value orientations, implicit in the analysis of international migration of professionals and scientists can be identified, Acute individualism, intense nationalism and committed professionalism. He explored that the process, needs and the interests of the migrant individuals, the nation states involved are inextricably entertained. In his context of analysis secondary data is used to illuminate the migration of Indian scientists & professionals.

Shah, Nasra (1991) others conducted three surveys between 1977-81 and also data derived from census on the "Asian Women Workers in Kuwait" attempted the occupational characteristics, house-hold conditions and wages of Asian women in Kuwait, they emphasized mostly on Non-Maids (Teachers, Nurses and Secretaries) compared with Kuwaiti nationals and Arab counterparts. The policies of the sending countries is examined and future flow of labour. Kuwait has a policy to reduce alien labour and encourage indigenous labour. They observed the Asian males are more in demand in Kuwait.

Looney (1992) studied the impact of Arab vs. Asian expatriate workers on Kuwait's development is examined through application of the "Dutch Disease Model" and regression analysis of Kuwait's economic sectorial outputs, results suggest that Asian workers made weak positive contribution to agricultural output and fishing while Arab workers made strong contributors to the food production, textiles, paper products, petroleum refining and private services. Overall the Asian expatriate work force made much less positive contribution to the countries expansion than expatriate workers, indicating that Arabization coincides with Kuwait's economic objectives.

Sen Kasturi (1986) in her Ph.D. dissertation "Migrants from the Indian sub-continent and the Kuwait labour market: economic, political and social determinants" expressed that the transformation in the structure and composition of labour force in the Gulf in general and in Kuwait in particular reveals an increasing pre-dominance of non-Arabs over Arab migrants in the labour market since 1970s. Migration of Indians played an important role in this transformation. The analysis confined predominantly to statistical and historical studies. It stressed a phenomena which is historically and structurally determined, have created a number of increasing institutionalized misconception on the nature, role and implications of the transformation in the ethnic composition of the migrant labour force. An attempt is made to evaluate in this work the origin and implication of this mode of analysis, utilising Kuwait and the Indian sub-continent migrant presence there as the case in point. The role and function of the Indian sub-continent migrants on the Kuwait's political economy and on alternative perspective is proposed.

All Ghabra, Shafeeq Nazam (1987) Ph.D. work on "Palestinians in Kuwait. The family and politics of survival" attempted the conservative approach and attitude of the Palestinian families in exile after the war of 1948. Basically, they established social net works in Saudi Arabia, Qatar, Lebanon, Jordan and the united states. The intelligentsia and the peasantry are studied in two different chapters.

The Palestinian family into a cross national entity is also discussed. For example, one family with brothers and sisters along with their spouses children and relatives are scattered cross national entity, each carrying different citizenship papers and travel documents.

The Palestinians in Kuwait established a strong base of "Kuwait's Palestinian villages" since 1976. In sum, the study demonstrates that, in the face of displacement, divisive attack and insecurity, the Palestinians have employed primarily the family as a basic means of survival.

Al Najadah, Abdulla Fozan Al Fozan (1989), Ph.D thesis, "social change and Alienation in Kuwait", highlighted the Kuwaiti society, its economic, political and social structure before the oil exploration, followed by the development of oil resource and society change using the scales of straining and Richardson levels of alienation in Kuwait are then measured and the results given. New scales are specifically developed. The study highlighted the new areas of future research possibilities.

Al-Otaiba, Obaid Srour, Ph.D thesis (1988) on "Shopping Centre Development and Consumer Behaviour in Kuwait", the study explores the high revenue produced due to discovery of oil have led to a growth in national affluence reflected in increased consumer wealth and education. Greater contacts with the west has led to a degree of westernization. These two factors resulted in a new shopping order and consumer behaviour for more luxury goods.

The shopping habits of the consumer have a serious impact on the traditional retail system. The new shopping markets have extra sophisticated and infrastructural facilities. The National Master Plan has proposed a number of new large scale purpose built shopping centres to meet the anticipated demand by the end of the century due to a rise in population.

The study has undertaken three different surveys to study the shopping complexes and the consumer behaviour, the finding illustrate the degree of success and prospects of the existing commercial complexes, whose popularity augers well for the future of the proposed larage scale purpose built shopping centres.

Al-Moosa, Abdul Rasool (1988) presented a paper in the journal for social sciences titled "Salaried Employment: A Consequence of Urbanisation in Kuwait". He emphasized the economic boon in Kuwait brought about by oil revenue spawned rapid urbanisation and the establishment of new institutions. The development of salaried employment as a significant aspect of social and economic change, gave rise to new social norms causing changes in interpersonal relations and individual aspirations. Traditional occupations in Kuwait created interdependence between the individual and the family, have lost their significance. This has got overpowered by the salaried employment. The various changes accompanying and the urban problems are identified and examined in this paper.

Abdo, Mohammed Fawzi (1988), Ph.D thesis, "The Urbanisation of Kuwait since 1950: Planning Progress and Issues". In the modern Kuwait master plans were prepared by the specialist early in 1951. They were aimed for the coming three decades to follow. Continuous changes in the built environment often progressed faster than the plans anticipated. Successive plans were gradually adopted with wider scope.

The thesis examined the process of Urbanisation and the Planning in Kuwait, with issues related to demographic, economic and public policies. The study showed how various plans have responded to specific charges and circumstances. An assessment of the emerging urban environment in the Kuwait city's central part, the hub of government and business activities is explored.

The study concluded, that the four decades of planning effort in Kuwait was neither poorly concerned and realised nor ideal. It is instead, the outcome of a combination of dynamic and often predictable forces, public policy considerations and changes, and certain constraints on planning, both in terms of its physical as well as practical aspects, the study, finally is a documentation of the making of urban Kuwait during its modern era.

Kabbra Abdurahaman Haitham Shoukat (1988) Ph.D thesis, "Islamic Banking Case Study of Kuwait".

In the aftermath of the islamic resurgence movement, the call for abolition of interest, the profit and loss schemes gained momentum. Although, the operation of islamic banks is outlined, but the implications of abolishing interest in a specific economy is hot studied earlier. Hence, this was examined for Kuwait's banking and its economy, a number of recommendations based on the findings are made, the advantage and disadvantages of interest free banking with reference to Kuwait is discussed.

Alshayeji, Abdullah Khalifah (1988) Ph.D thesis "Democratization in Kuwait: The National Assembly as a strategy for political survival". The study is a focus on the hybrid Kuwaiti political system which combines a powerful hereditary with a limited democratic practice embodied by the National Assembly, which developed as part of a political institutional strategy to lessen and contain Kuwait's acute vulnerability. The study chronicles the rise and demise of the National Assembly and concentrates on its role, structure, legitimacy and mechanisms as well as its relevance, and overall contribution to the Kuwaiti political system.

The study addresses issues like, the power of the Amir to suspend the parliamentary body any time, why the Al-Sabah family initiated the democratic reforms and that Kuwait is the only pioneer country to do in the whole of the Arabian Peninsula. It also envisages how Kuwait laid the ground work for the relatively stable political transition from families patrimonial kinship society to a modern nation state and why the legitimacy of the ruling Al-sabah family is not only unchallenged but entrenched after some two hundred and thirty two years of uninterrupted rulership.

The study argues that the Kuwaiti National Assembly provided a useful arena in which elite interaction could unfold peacefully and in which elite co-operation, in managing the politics of a society undergoing rapid socio-economic changes could develop.

Finally, the study highlights the Kuwaiti parliamentary experience can be appreciated only when viewed as part of a political strategy aimed at lessening Kuwait's vulnerability and working external and internal threats. Besides, the need to adapt a certain western democratic experience, while retaining its traditional, deep rooted islamic teachings and its entrenched tribal heritage.

"Crime among immigrants: A sociological study of crime in Kuwait." is studied by Bu Rasheed, Adel, J. (1988). The study was an attempt to investigate the possible socio-economic and political factors integrating to criminal behaviour. The respondents were drawn from the central jail of Kuwait. The responses with regard to Age, education, marital status, duration of stay, income level, staying with family or alone were subjected to various statistical analysis.

The finding show that compared to the Kuwaiti offenders, immigrant offenders were older, less educated, less often accompanied by their wives, have lower levels of income, live in heterogeneous areas, and were more socially isolated than the Kuwaitis. Both immigrants and Kuwaiti offenders scored high on the "anomy scale". Non-Kuwaiti, non-Arab immigrants committed more crimes compared to non-Kuwaiti Arab immigrants.

"Women, labour force participation, and equality a study of Educated Women in Kuwait" was undertaken by Al-Dhafiri, Abdul Wahab Mohammad (1987). About 293 university female graduates were interviewed. Based on the past research which has shown that educated Kuwaiti women are more work oriented and large numbers of college students are expected to enter the labour force about ten hypothesis were tested, six of them were proven false.

The study has shown, house-hold composition, socio-economic and sex role orientation were final to be major factors affecting the likelihood of Kuwaiti women entering the labour force. A majority of the educative women still hold conservative attitudes about sex-appropriate behaviour. Legal equality was not an important issue for educated Kuwaiti women.

"The International labour migration to Kuwait, its impacts, determinants and future prospects" is studied by "Maylah Mohammad Hussan" (1987), his work was related to deal with, after the emergence of oil the causes and consequences of the labour migration to Kuwait, the labour demand and supply in the state, and the economic theory of labour mobility regression technique was used on the obtained and available data to examine the migration hypothesis and to test the human capital model in the context of supply of immigrant labour time and earnings determination in Kuwait's labour market. The explanation power of the conventional model of the supply of labour time is higher among natives than among immigrants, suggesting that several restrictions are imposed on the employment of the latter. These have resulted in a segmented labour market within which the earnings differential between natives and immigrants is fairly wide.

Within an overall assessment of the immigrants role in Kuwait's economy, the study postulates that immigrants are brought to the country to make good the aggregate labour deficit, to fill jobs which locals are either untrained for, or anxious to avoid, and to stimulate the domestic economic activity. Not with standing, their impact on long term development prospects is limited. This together with the shrinking oil resource, is expected to reduce the demand for migrant labour in the foreseeable future.

Al-Gazali, Essa Mohammad (1989) presented his Ph.D thesis on "Human Resource Policies and the welfare state administration in Kuwait. He emphasized, the issue of human resource potential in the wake of oil exploration, the social and political issue aroused in the third world countries, Kuwait had a comfortable financial situation prior to the oil discovery it had a traditional culture, the overwhelming socio-economic transformation initiated since 1946. The manpower problem to aim economic diversification came as a major policy issue. The native labour force was limited in size, neither effectively developed nor efficiently utilized. The result being foreign labour import.

The Kuwaiti public service is over staffed, hence it neglects other potential areas of development. The socio-cultural background of the Kuwaitis encouraged a few selective occupations, priority service, hence, except the service sector, other economic sectors were filled by expatriates, the whole pattern has been reinforced by the nature of the political system of the country, and by the "rentier" nature of its economy, which depended on the generation of oil income and his income access directly of the state. The state in turn disburses the income on welfare activities, including the guarantee of a public post for every Kuwait citizen who desires such a position.

"The composition and growth of the labour force in Kuwait" was studied by Allak, Mohammed (1989). The massive oil revenue of the Kuwait created a great demand for expatriate labour due to shortfall of the indigenous workers, this resulted in excess of non-Kuwaitis in majority. The two factors of indigenous labour supply was their small size and low labour participation, secondly due to very low female participation and the young age structure of the Kuwait population.

REFERENCES

Abdo Mohammad Fowzi (1988), "The urbanisation of Kuwait since 1950: Planning Progress and Issues", Ph.D Thesis.

Al-Dafiri, Abdul Wahad Mohammad (1987), "Women, Labour Force perticipation, and Equality : A study for educated women in Kuwait", Ph.D Thesis.

Al-Ghabra Shafeeq Nazem (1987), "Palestinions in Kuwait: The family and politics of servival", Ph.D Thesis.

Al-Ghazali, Essa Mohammed (1989), "Human Resource Policies and the Welfare State Administration in Kuwait", Ph.D Thesis.

Al-Moosa-Abdul Rasool (1988), Salaried employment - A consequences of urbaniation in Kuwait", Journal of Social Sciences, 16, pp. 121-141.

Al-Moosa-Kerith Mclahn (1985), "Immigrant Labour in Kuwait".

Al-Najadah, Abdulla Fozan Al Fozan (1989), "Social Change and Alienation in Kuwait", Ph.D Thesis.

Al-Ofariba, Obaid Srour (1988), "Shopping Centre Development and Consumer Behaviour in Kuwait", Ph.D Thesis.

Al-Sahhaf Habeeb (1990), "Human Resource Management in Kuwait", Ph.D Thesis.

Al-Shayeji, Abdullah Khalifah (1988), "Democratization in Kuwait: The National Assembly as a strategy for political survival", Ph.D Thesis.

Allah Mohammad (1989), "The composition and growth of the labour force in Kuwait", Ph.D Thesis.

Beaujean Gornier J. (1966), "Geography of Population", Longman, London, p. 171.

Boque D.J. (1969). op cit.

Boque. J.J. (1969), "Principles of Demography", Willey, New York, p. 752.

Brandes S.H. (1975), "Migration, Leinship and Community", Academic Press, New York.

Bu-Rasheed Add J. (1988), "Crime among immigrants: A sociological study of crime in Kuwait", Ph.D Thesis.

Clark and Moore (1980), "Residential Mobility and Public Policy", Urban Affairs - Annual Review, p. 19, New York.

Cleanson and Eqaro (1972), "Migration in Tanzania" - A review based in the 1967 population census - Research notes No.1", University of Dar-es-Salam.

Eisenstedt S.N. (1953), "Analysis of patterns of immigration and absorption of immigrants-Population studies", 7, pp. 167-80.

Farah Tawfic. E. (1989), "Population Culture and Development in a Rentier State: The case of Kuwait", Journal of African and Asian Studies, 24, 1-2 Jan - April, pp.106-113.

Ghabra Shaffeq (1991), "The Iraqi occupation of Kuwait - An eyewitness account", Journal of Palestinian studies, 20, pp. 112-125.

Grigg D.B. (1977), "E.G. Revenstein and the Laws of Migration", Journal of historical geography, 3, pp. 41-54.

Hagerstrand T. (1957), "Migration and Area - Survey of a sample of Sweidsh migration fields and hypothetical consideration of their genesis", In Hannesberg, pp.27-158.

Jackson J.A. (1969) (ed), "Migration, Sociological Studies 2", Cambridge University Press, Cambraidge.

Jansen C.J. (1970), "Reading in the Sociology of Migration", Pargamon, Oxford.

Kabbra Abdurrahman Haithman Shoukat (1988), "Islamic Banluing: A case study of Kuwait", Ph.D Thesis.

Khalidi Walid (1991), "The Gulf crisies - Origin and Consequences", Journal of Palestinian Studies, 20, pp. 5-28.

Kosinshi L.A. and Protherto R.M (1975), "People in the move, Studies in internal migration", Metheun, London.

Kurup B.S. "Determinants and consequences of migration", Sharif Bhownisk - Economic and political weekly, April 7, 1984, pp. 589-590.

Leela Gulati, "Male migration to middle east and the impact on the family - some evidence from Kerala", Economic and Political Weekly, Dec. 4-31, 1983, pp. 2217-2225.

Lewis G.J. (1974), "Human Migration", Unit 9, Regional Analysis and Development, Open University Press, Milton Keynes.

Looney R.E. (1992), "Manpower option in a small labour importing state: The influence of ethnic composition in Kuwaits development", International migration, 30-2 June, pp. 175-200.

Lowry I.S. (1966), "Migration and Metropolitan Growth", Two analytical models, chandler, San Fransisco.

Mangalam J.J. (1968), "Human Migration", University of Kentuchy Press, Lerington.

Manolo-1-Abella, "Labour migration from south and south east Asia - some policy Issues", International Labour Review, Vol. 123, No. 4, July-August, 1984, pp. 491-506.

Mathew E.T., Gopinath Nair, "Socio-economic characteristics of Emigrants and Emigrants households - A case study of two villages in Kerala", Economic and Political Weekly, pp. 1141-1153.

Maylah Mohammad Hassan (1987), "The International labour migration to Kuwait, its impacts, determinants and future prospects", Ph.D Thesis.

Mongalam J.J. (1968), "Human Migration", University of Kenturkey Press.

Mowad Galal Abdulla (1987), "Urbanisation and labour migration in the Arab countries of the Gulf', Journal of the Gulf and Arabrian penisula studies, 1987, 13, 51, July.

Nagi-Mustafa H. (1988), "Consequences of International Migration for Work to the oil rich countries in the middle east - A political economy perspective".

Oomen T.K. (1989), "India - Vrain drain of the migration of Talent", International Migration, 27, 3 September, pp. 411-425.

Pertha S. Ghosh, "Our Gulf policy - some nagging doubts", Mainstream, Sept. 8, 1990, p. 11.

Prakash B.A. "Impact of Foreign remittances - A case study of Chavakkad village in Kerala", Economic Political Weekly, pp.1106-1111.

Pryer, R.J. (1979), "Internal Migration and Urbanisation".

Rizwanut Isalam (1980), "Export of manpower from Bangla Desh to middle east countries — The impact of remittance money on household expenditure", NFRHRD, Dhaka.

Sen-Kasturi (1986), "Migrants from Indian sub-continent and the Kuwait labour market — Economic, Political and Social Determinants", Ph.D Thesis.

Shah Nasra, M.Al-Qudsi-Sulayaman S, and Shajkh Maqdoom. A (1991), "Asian Women Workers in Kuwait", International migration review, 25.

Sharma P.C. (1978), "Population Migration", A Selected Bibliographical research guide 1972-77, Public administration series.

Show R.P. (1975), "Migration Theory and Fact", A Review and Bibliography of current literature.

Show, R.P. (1975). op cit.

Simmie J.M. (1972), "The sociology of Information Migration", Centre for Environmental Studies, London.

Soman H. Chowdhry (1986), "Labour migration to the middle east: An Asian perspective", Asian Economic Review, April 1, 1986, pp. 43-73.

Spencer R.F. (1970), "Migration and Anthropology", University of Washington Press, Seattle.

Todaro M.P. (1969), "A model of labour migration and urban unemployment in less developed countries", American Economic Review, 59, pp. 138-48.

Weinberg A.A. (1961), "Migration and Belonging: A study of mantal health and personal adjustment in Israel", Martinus Nishoff, The Hague.

Willis, K.G. (1974), "Problems in Migration Analysis", Saxon House, Farnborough.

Word R.J. (1980), "Migration, Myth and Magic in Papua New Guinea, Australian", Geographical Studies, 18, pp. 119-34.

Zelinshy W. (1971), "The hypothesis of the mobility transition", Geographical Review, 61, pp. 219-49.

2

AN OVERVIEW OF INDIAN LABOUR EMIGRATION TO SOUTH WEST ASIA

Indians are found almost in every Asian country in particular and the world in general. As traders, travellers, labourers and they have been moving in varied directions. India facilitated migrations easy to both 'Comers' and 'Goers'. Indian policy always had been peace and cooperation, People visiting India were treated as Guests. The Indian tradition and culture is Human and it always welcomed refugees, visitors, conquerors and others. The shape, location, the geographical setting, the fertile land, the natural barriers played a vital role to practice and promote the Indian ideology. There were also occasions where in Indians migrating to the different parts of the world, for various political, religions and social census. Religious ethos, limited transport technology, poverty, idealogy of peace and tolerance, strong patriorism, sufficient resources for food, shelter and clothing and overall a rich cultural heritage and hearth of India with a very long standing history strongly bound the Indians close to the bossom of Mother India.

Indian emigration in search of acquiring wealth initiated by a small number of people on their own to the neighbouring countries dates back to 18th century (Weiner 1982). As emperor Ashoka the great Indian king propagated Buddhism to its neighbouring countries. India established at first, religious propaganda migration, learned people, monks, Gurus were sent under the patronage of the king and noblemen to spread the message of world peace and humanity to the different parts of the world.

A major thrust of Indian emigration occurred after the abolition of slavery in the British territories in 1833-34. The gap created by the slaves was filled by Indian 'Indentured Labour'. In return for a passage and a wage, the emigrant undertook to work for a specified employer for three to five years (Sandhu 1969). This type of bonded labour system was opposed and strongly condemned by Justice Beaumont the former Chief Justice of British Guyana. He described "the indentured as a monstrous, rotten system, rooted upon slavery, growth in its stale soil, emulating its worst abuses and only more dangerous because it presented itself under false colours whereas slavery (had) the brand of infamy written upon its forehead" (Sandhu 1969). Subsequently indentured system was abolished by the British Government in 1916.

International labour and other associated movements basically occurred in three phases, the first phase between 1840 and 1930, trans-occanic exodus European of about 0.52 million came in light (U N Department of Economic and Social Affairs 1979). During the same period, about 3 million Indians migrated to Burma, Ceylon, Malaysia, Fiji, Mauritius, Trinidad and Tobago, Surinam, Guyana, Jamaica, South and East Africa. During the second phase, 1930-50, the world witnessed the world wars which shook the nations. Heavy loss of life and property economic depression, social, political and cultural transgression created a wide spectrum of human misery. A new international policy and understanding was adopted in the form of diplomacy. Fleeing the country, prisoners of war, refugees, partition of nations, decolonisation, declaration of independence by a number of suppressed colonial nations created a heavy exodus of people from one place to another. The Asian and African continent witnessed a new Geo-polito-economic scenario, various cooperative organisations between nations for peace and prosperity were chalked out. The redistribution of population coupled with cultural and ideological exchanges witnessed under this phase.

The human migrations were occurring on a large scale, it is observed that the human loss due to wars, drought, disease (cholera and plague) particularly the atomic bombing on Hiroshima and Nagasaki (Japan) left a trail of death and devastation, scores of men, women, children were handicapped or seriously injured. The after math of the war led to a fear psychosis and migration to safer nations: between 1950 and 1980 the world witnessed a third phase of post war migration. The United States admitted 10.8 million immigrants, Canada 2.5 million. Western Europe had 6.5 million migrant workers and as many dependents upto 1980, Middle East had 3 million migrant workers and one million dependents. South America had about 4 million migrant workers, West Africa 1.3 million and South Africa 0.3 million, Australia had 2.1 million workers, New Zealand 0.4 million (1971). In this third phase of 30 years duration about 3 million Indians migrated to Nepal, Sri Lanka, Malaysia and Singapore (Bohning 1984).

Bohning (1984) estimates the global stock of migrant workers as on 1980 to be atleast 19.7 million to 21 million. Adding the undocumented migrants he speculates the figures to be between 25 to 30 million. But the U N Deptt. of International Economic & Social Affairs 1982, has calculated contract migrants and undocumented migrant to be around 50.55 million in 1981, of which 60% originated from developing countries and one third of these are Indians.

Indian Emigration

Majority of Indians emigrated as indentured labour to Fiji, the West Indies and Mauritius to work in the sugar plantation and for the construction of Railways in Uganda (Tinker 1977). The labour shortage faced by Ceylonese Sri Lanka and Malayan (Malaysian) plantation owners led to another system of labour recruitment known as 'Kangani' system. Huge amount is advanced and which tied workers under debt bondage, planters preferred to compete for labour with offers of large cash advance instead of payment of higher wages. Although Kangani system encouraged and filled the labour gap of the plantation workers in Ceylon and Malaya it has come under severe attack due to its system of recruitment for gross violation of law. This system was consequently banned in 1938 by the Indian Government.

The Indian labour in South-East Asia and East Africa filled up the gap of labour shortage, but the Indian migrant was doomed in disease ridden conditions to provide sugar, coffee and tea and other raw materials for the industries of Europe, they also ended up having only a precarious basis as a low status and disrupted minority in the societies they entered and sometimes with no citizenship at all (Omvedt 1980).

In contrast to this, Indians who moved into these territories as non-labourers, as merchants, traders, vendors and financiers made good of their visits. They fared so well that they become the economic anchors. The Nattukottai Chettiars. In their role as financial intermediaries seemed to have acquired more wealth in Malaya, Burma and Ceylon than any other Indian Community. The wealth of 1300 families of Nattukottai Chettiars, was assessed at 60 million. After independence their wealth was nationalised and they did not receive any compensation. Indians as clerks and technical personnel also fared well. Sikhs as policemen, caretakers, guards, also made good fortunes, (Ghai and Ghai 1970), Sandhu 1969) and (Chakravarthy 1979). M.C. Madhavan (1985) estimates that 3 million Indians migrated to different countries between 1800-1945 of these 2.2 million went to Ceylon, Burma and Malaysia. 42000 to East Africa and 50,000 to United States, U.K. and Canada. After World War II as many as 750000 Indian emigrants were residing in the developed countries UK (44%), US ((26%), Canada (14%) W. Europe (excluding UK) (11%), and Australia (5%), Ermisch (1983).

The Indian born emigrants are estimated to be 5.0 to 5.5 million (2.2 to 2.7 million excluding Nepal) spread all over the world by the year 1981. This also amouts to 0.73 to 0.81 per cent of the population of India, Madhavan (1985). The population of Indian origin calculated by various sources amounts to 13.2-13.8 million Indians residing all over the world, Jain (1982). Estimates of Indian Origin for various years is given by Nahundan (1950), Kondapi (1951), Tinker (1977).

The growth of labour force in middle east within a span of five years (1975-80) increased to the tune of 2.55 lakhs, nearly twice its existing labour force. Kuwait had an increase of 1.52 lakhs accounting for one half increase. As much as sixty-one thousand and forty-five thousand labourers were added to Bahrain and Qater respectively. Bahrain had the highest per cent growth rate (79%) followed by Qater (68%) UAE (66%) and Kuwait (51%). Birlas and Sinclair, (1980) Naxil Choucri (1983).

The annual contract migrant outflow between 1976-1983 shows that between 1978-1982 heavy trend of migration is noticed from the south, south-east and east Asian countries. In south Asia, Pakistan sent 42 thousand people in the year 1976 where only 4 thousand Indians migrated, by the next year the former sent 1.4 lakh people and latter only 23,000 Pakistan maintained above one lakh migrants henceforth and by 1980, India picked up by sending 23.6 lakh people and retained the trend upto 1983. However Pakistan also had about 1.5 lakh people migrated annually. The figures for Bangladesh and Sri Lanka received below one lakh for any given year. (National Statistics).

In South Asia and East Asia the competition was between the Koreans and the Philippines. In the race, Philippines overpowered the Koreans and they in 1982-83 out numbered all other countries in the world by sending 3.5 lakhs and 3.3 lakhs respectively.

Total manpower of Asia in the year 1981 in the Middle East account for 1,95,72,000 Demery (1983). But the World Bank study puts upto 732340 persons, Birks and Sinclair (1980) calculated as 820580 people. It is also noticed that the Pakistani's amongst the Asians are the highest followed by Philippines and Indians.

South Asians migrants in the Gulf are preferred than Europeans and Americans since they do not demand high wages even for specialized jobs. They do not lead a costly way of life, speak good english, have good health, and are generally bachelors. Besides, the Gulf countries have no fears of protest or threat of withdrawal from the Asian Governments as their labour problem is partially solved, remittances increase the balance of payments besides growing goodwill of OPEC for oil import and other diplomatic ties and improved relations.

Indian Government would not allow elsewhere the ill-treatment meted to its citizens. But in the Gulf it has a policy of tolerance and encourages migration and entertains remittances. The policy is not to discourage the professionals either to migrate in addition to the skilled and the semi-skilled labour power migrating from India.

It is observed by 1975 that the Palestinian percentage in Kuwait and Saudi Arabia was at the top, where Asians were the least. Elsewhere in the Middle East the Asians dominated the Palestinians. The latter with their weak political base and insecure socio-economic traits have become world wanderers. The Arab world welcomes them and is desirous of keeping their spirits high to get back to their home country. With attractive economic packages they have percolated into Kuwait (40%), Saudi Arabia (34%) and Qater (18%). Although the former has maximum Palestinians it has also provided room for Europeans, Americans and Asians.

The inflow of migrant labour to that of the native labour in the Gulf by the year 1975 shows that the United Arab Emirates, Qater and Kuwait had 95% and 71% respectively. Oman and Bahrain had 45% and 40% respectively. The former state had its native labour migrated elsewhere for higher wages.

The demand for migrant labour in the Gulf was basically to facilitate the oil exploration projects, executed by the developed nations. The enormous labour of South Asia was willing to contribute its skill and expertise in lieu of handsome wages. The gulf elites in order to create welfare states opposed the redistribution of political power supported the policies of wealth redistribution in the form of free education, healthcare, drinking water and low cost housing facilities to its citizens. Majority of their people were in the administrative positions. Hence, in order to maintain and smooth the economy they encouraged migrant labour in construction work as teachers, doctors, accountants, managers and technical personnel for a temporary stay and hope that their own native citizens would one day themselves manage all these services.

The rich Gulf states with their enormous oil potential and financial deposits had no dearth of money but that of labour. These states were also attempting to diversify their economy and reduce their dependence on oil exports by investing in other industries. The migrant labour became imminent in the Gulf States also because of low national population and labour force to cope with the demand for labour. Besides their native population was not having any skill or education to take up the required jobs. The 1975 national labour participation of the five Gulf States was only 30%. It had 40% of its population below 15 years of age and very few of their women fold undertook employment. In all the five Gulf States had a total population of 3.8 million, but only 1.5 million were the local citizens.

The rural folk of the Gulf labour particularly Oman in the year 1975 had its 40000 workers in agriculture and about nearly the same number migrated to other Gulf states for higher wages. This also created a gap in the urban modern sector. Kuwait and United Arab Emirates also has a sizable labour in the rural economy.

Gulf countries have their own developmental programmes. Investments were made in banking, aluminium plants, flour processing, dry docks, oil refineries, hotels, airports, roadways and communication, construction of schools, hospitals etc. Immigrants are brought to the country to make good the aggregate labour deficit to fill jobs which locals are either untrained for of anxious to avoid, or to stimulate the domestic economy. Initially the labour was brought for construction followed by maintenance and development Weinar (1982).

Arab employees earn high income with little or no work, but receive very high salaries. They become silent partners to the foreign investors. Since Gulf states emphasize that their citizens only own business, foreign investors search silent partners to make good of their investment. The Rich Emir Families including the rulers own hotels, banks, housing complexes and factories with foreign collaborations.

Half of the Gulf citizens are literates in traditional, orthodox and conservative education based on Koranic schools. The higher education (University) does not prepare the students for meeting their domestic modern Industrial economy and future perspective planning to lead their states towards developments. Few bright scholars attend foreign schooling and research activities. But their contribution to have status in terms of developmental activities is not seen.

A culture of heavy consumerism is evident in the Gulf states, with a different type of education and free education, health care, low housing and free hand in business made the locals to have a high disposable income. Conservation of resources is never thought of in these states. It appears that the locals are consumers and the expatriates are the producers. All the developmental activities are shouldered by the immigrants.

In the early states of economic development in the middle-east Arab labour surplus countries dominated the labour market to a tune of 12% labour force upto 1970 (Ahmad Mansoor 1982) and 25% in the year 1975. The South Yemanis migrated to Saudi Arabia and Sudanese to Egypt. Egyptians went to the other countries of the Gulf, Palestinians and Jordanians also migrated in greater number though no single group dominated the labour market. The stock of expatriate workers during 1970-75 swelled from 880000 to 1800000. Most of the migration took place between 1973-75. The Indians and Pakistani migrant workers in the year 1975 constituted to 18%. The Pakistani's increased from 200000 in 1975 to 500000 in 1977 and 1.25 million in 1979 (Akbar Mahmood 1981).

In the early stages intra-regional migration dominated within the Arab countries. Egyptians and Jordanians migrated as administrators, teachers and professionals. Semi-skilled workers from south Yamen, Sudan and Jordan migrated to Saudi Arabia. The Palestinians formed separate group and received special treatment. However no single migrant group dominated. In 1970 of 6.5 lakh emigrant workers 71000 were Palestinians, 94000 Egyptians and 92000 Jordanians together formed only 12% of the migrant workers.

The second phase of migration began after 1973. Owing to huge investments in the development projects for the faster economic growth new vista of migration stream of workers started. The Arab world experienced large scale adjustments in their labour forces. The 1973-75 migration profile was composed of skilled and semi-skilled labourers from Egypt and Jordan to large extent, skilled labour from Algeria, Tunisia and Morocco. The Asians were migrating in specified professions viz construction, service and manufacturing sector. In the year 1975, three-quarter of the total migrant workers were from neighbouring Arab countries. Asians share being 20% increased to 30% in 1980 (Sinclair 1979).

The Asians in the Gulf labour market started their predominate role in the third phase of middle east labour migration around 1975. The share of Asian labour was 20-30-36% in the years 1975-80-85 respectively. A study of the World Bank predicted the foreign work force in the region would decline from 65% in 1975 to 52% in 1985. However if forecasted the share from India would grow from 21.6% in 1975 to 25.6% in 1985. Workers from far East would soar from 14 to 10.5% during the same period.

Pakistan has sent the largest number of workers to the middle east, because of its physical proximity and Pan Islamic solidarity. By the year 1975 about 200000 Pakistani labour existed in the middle east. During 1981 it swelled to over one million. Indian labour followed next with more than a million in the year 1981. Together Asian countries sent 300000 labourers to the Gulf states in 1974 Keeley (1980) and by the year 1981 more than 2 million Asians constituted the migrant labour of middle east.

South east and far east asian countries mainly Korea, Thailand, Philippines and Bangladesh also sent their labour to the middle east. However, their presence in 1974-75 was very low. By the year 1982 about one lakh Bangladeshi's Ali et al. (1981). Two lakhs each Thais and Koreans and about five lakh Philippines were scatered all over the middle east (Sirgeldin et al.).

The statistics available are mostly official. The non-illegal migrants are yet unknown. The data does not include skill-wise distribution of workers. It is also noticed that the employers choice of recruiting labour has always been changing. First Pakistanis, Indians were highly preferred. Later labour from East and South-east Asian got into demand. This is because of their low wage demand. Scores of Indonesians, Malays etc. are also found all over the middle eastern countries. Data for which is not immediately available.

Yet another drawback of the data is the no-record of the return migrants. Thailand has endorsed more freedom for the private recruitment agencies, as such the official figures are distorted. Different migrant workers of different countries have different sources have varying duration of stay. Since the migration is circulatory in nature and it is likely that substantial return flow occur alongside the outflows recorded. The contract labour the renewals, the re-entrants, the step migrants all together distort the real picture so as to make concrete analysis and interpretation.

Pattern of Remittances

The remittances received by India and Pakistan predominate the other Asian countries. Sri Lanka received the least. During the year 1980, India received as much as about three thousand million US dollars (Gulati & Mody, 1983).

The Gross Domestic investment rate has declined for most of the countries except for Philippines and Sri Lanka. Gross domestic savings as a percentage of GDP has increased for all countries except Bangladesh and the increase has been substantial for Korea, Philippines, Thailand and India. The position of the balance of payments could have been much precarious had there been no remittance and particularly India has avoided a bigger crisis.

The economic effects of the labour migration in the Middle East for selected Asian countries in analysed. It shows that the remittances have played a very crucial role in strengthening the economy. Net flow of foreign aid in real terms has declined in the sevnties and the remittances have been higher for most countries. Bangladesh and

Pakistan show remittances much higher than overall domestic saving. Positively this has opened a plethora of developmental activities in these countries.

According to a world bank report (1981) the inflow of workers remittances in Asian rose from US $200 million in 1968 to US $3900 million in 1978. The report further assess that India over a period of 1967-79 found its value of remittances increased by 19.4%. Pakistan between 1972-79 by 34.6%, Bangladesh between 1975-78 by 64.4%, Korea between 1967-79 by 11.7% by 1980 the Asian countries remittances totalled to US $7300 million.

During the year 1979 India earned $3.2 billion in foreign remittances of which $ 1.6 billion was from Middle East (Weiner 1982) Pakistan received $ 15.5 million in 1972-73 and it rose to $ 2.1 billion in 1981-82 i.e. 8% of its GNP Grilani et al. (1981). It also showed the remittances account for 40% from middle east of the total foreign exchange earnings and finances 86% of its trade deficit.

Korea received $ 2 billion from middle east in compulsory remittances during 1978 (Keeley 1980). According to Abella (1984) in 1980 alone the Asian countries amounted total remittances to $ 6 billion or 16% of their combined GNP. Pakistan (8.8%) Korea (3.4%), Sri Lanka (3.6%) and Bangladesh (3.4%).

Rizwanual Islam in his study entitled, "recession, employment and poverty in the developing countries of Asia" (Bangkok ARTEP 1984) found for Bangladesh the workers remittances compensated 14.6% of trade deficit in 1978 and rose to 2% by 1982. For India the remittances covered 49.4% of trade deficit in 1980 and 39.3% in 1981. Pakistani remittances rescued its trade deficit to as much as 62 and 75.8% in the years 1978 to 1982. Thailand remittances covered a smaller deficit proportion of about 12% in 1978 to 19.7% in 1980.

Asian labour sending countries adopted various liberal policy schemes to attract and utilize properly the workers remittances from abroad. In Bangladesh the 'Wage Earners Scheme' spent it 64% of remittances on imports of 40 items mainly raw material, machinery and to some extent the consumer and luxury items. This was during the period 1976-82. As much as 19000 takas (Bangladesh currency) were spent under this scheme.

India since 1975 encouraged the scheme of NRI (non-resident Indian) Account which provides a choice of opening either an external rupee account or foreign currency account. In whatever currency these deposits are made are exempted from Income and Property Tax and draw a slightly higher interest than domestic deposits. It also enables them to purchase a few items in greater demand like Scooters & Cars in a lesser duration. NRI amount is also entertained to purchase sophisticated machinery of medical treatment (cancer etc.) and import of english movies. In 1982 remittances paid into such accounts amounted to about 12% of total private transfers from abroad. Gulati (1983).

Remittances sent in foreign currency and foreign goods are purchased by the recipient has deflationary impact on the domestic economy of any country. Remittances used at non-traded goods or things like housing and real estates causes inflation. Studies on the remittance received households in Pakistan showed that 62% of migrant household expenditures are of consumption, 22% real estate and 13% investment (Gilani et al. 1981).

In Bangladesh household spent their remittances on purchase of land, construction of houses or repairs (Rizwaul Islam 1981) In Thailand substantial amounts are spent on house construction and renovation.

Official figures on remittances are bound to be under-estimates. Despite the encouragement by the host countries to encourge foreign exchange, unofficial channels are widely in use by the ignorant, low and middle income group migrants who make a substantial portion of migrants in the middle east. A lions share of this unofficial and un-accounted money is spent on unproductive feast, functions and festivals.

In the absence of the profit oriented projects and plans by the host countries due to its temporary phenomenon conceived and accepted by the migrants and the governments, the proper channel of debit and credit is highly distorted. Large portion of remittance money is not invested in the productive side but to immediate consumption. Major portion of the saving generated by the remittances are often used in luxury consumption or real estate purchase of land or housing.

Neither the short term nor long term strategies on remittances are drawn by the individuals nor the voluntary agencies (Bricks and

Sinclair 1979). Looking at several studies conducted, one would notice pervasive and widespread consequences of remittances both economic and social. A Bangladesh study (Islam 1980) shows migration is rather selective in the country's social context (among the middle and upper, income families) the additional remittance income served to increase income inequality. Studies by Shaheed (1981) and ILO/ARTEP (1983) reported that remittance income had generated a new class of 'neo-rich' migrant families resulting in new shifts in economic and social relations. The high propensity to consumer among the migrants and their families and correspondingly among non-migrant families through demonstration effect have led to inflationary pressure. (Sirajaldin 1983, Akbar: Mathews 1983).

The significance of remittances in the national economies of the Asian countries has been considerable. There is a sure contribution of remittances in the overall growth performances of these countries. It is observed that not much research on the macro-economic implications of remittances is strictly studied. The effects are pervasive, not much organised research have taken place in delicating various economic effects of migrants for these countries. The economic effects of labour migration as felt on a few select Asian countries in middle east in the year 1980 have been analysed.

In terms of the net inflow of foreign capital during the year 1980 for the asian countries declined and remittances were in comfortable position particularly that of Pakistan and India. The investment reserves, the savings and the GDP show a secure and secluded economic profile of these countries.

India's remittances equalled to 30% of the exports add the balance of payments compensated to a tune of 43.6% and on goods and services it rescued to as much as 46.5% during the fiscal year 1980-81. (IMF and Reserve Bank of India 1984).

It is difficult to envisage the proportion of savings remitted by the migrants. It was found by weiner (1982) that an average Indian sends one third or one half of his income to the motherland from the Middle Eastern countries. The Indian US migrants remitted one third of their savings in 1969 (Rose et al. 1969). The other savings are invested in host countries by the Indians. Occasionally when these people return to India a certain jewellary, consumer durable and small cash is brought by them.

It if further noticed that the remittance savings of households in India particularly that of Keralites doubled between 1970-80 and reduced in inequality in income distribution of the households. However most of its savings were spent on consumption, purchase of agricultural land, construction of new houses and education of children. Only 5% is used in stocks, bonds and commercial enterprises Nair (1983). The same source (reports that due to heavy migration of skilled artisans, the domestic artisan wages were quadrupled during 1973-84, the whole sale prices got doubled and the land values got soared to 32 times higher than what it had been in 1970's.

Employment Effects

The labour emigration for employment in middle east has its considerable impact on the senders country's labour, finance and goods and service markets. The labour market in terms of skill shortage and higher labour wages and huge remittances directed towards construction had shortage on certain fields particularly, domestic servants, plantation workers, sewage and sanitation workers, skilled, semi-skilled and un-skilled manual labour for construction etc. In addition to these the artisan community like carpenters, electricians, heavy equipment operators, para medical personnel, plumbers, lorry drivers, etc., created a certain stop-gap in most of the Asian countries. The professional and managerial sectors also were affected to a certain extent.

Irrespective of skill and labour shortage in the various sectors of the sender countries of Asia, the domestic unemployment front would recapitulate and compensate with lesser duration particularly India, Thailand and Sri Lanka fall under such category. Elsewhere the shortage did have its impact felt slightly on a larger scale.

Pakistan felt the labour shortage acute, to immediately fill up the gap, since 1973 the repercussions were significantly felt and were acute. Akbar (1981) reports skill shortages in consumption and manufacturing industries. Shortage of masons, carpenters, electricians welders and plumbers was noticed by Ahmad (1982).

Construction and manufacturing labour shortage was also felt in Philippines Stahl (1981), Bangladesh (Ali et al. 1979), and Korea Kiln (1982). In Philippines the shortage was readily compensated by the unemployed youth getting trained at the earliest to fill the gap reports (edita tan 1983). Siddiqui (1983) reports from Bangladesh that the 'increase in wages have lagged behind' increase in prices and there is no evidence to indicate that the general wage levels have been influenced by overseas employment'.

Korea felt the excess wage rose from 418% in construction to 448% in transport sectors between 1975-80, Abella (1982). A world bank report (1979) studied that an excess of female labour participation substituted for men between 1972-78. The increase in female labour was from 38% to 42.2%.

The impact of emigration of any country's economic growth and development has various implications. The size and characteristics of emigrants is related to the population growth, remittances and role of returnees on the developmental projects undertaken in the native country are some few factors.

Indian emigration population of reproductive age group and over all population growth showed a meagre impact. In one of the recent decades it experienced 2% of decennial population growth (during 1960's and 1970's the emigration and the population growth in India received 2.4 million and 2.2 million emigration as against 108 million and 136 million growth of popualtion respectively).

The work force migratory scenario of Indians in the year 1981 witnessed a million people in the middle east alone. The total of all the developed nations had about 800 thousand people. The absolute work-force of middle east was 600 thousand as against only 353 thousand of the combined developed countries.

Regarding the per cent of work force, the developed countries witnessed 45% in work force and 55% dependents, the figures got tilted for the developing countries. In fact, 58% of work force in the developing countries could go upto 65% if official count and the unofficial or undocumented numbers are combined. Middle East which shows 63% of work force can add another 10% correctly to this figure after adding the undocumented list.

The occupational categories are classified into four types. The professional and technical personnel found highly comfortable ranging anywhere between 50-80% in the developed countries for the Indians. The low percentage in the developing nations for the same category cannot be deemed due to lack of interest of the professionals, but by 1981 these nations particularly middle East has discouraged

Indians in this category. But after exhausting the Arab professionals if it has encouraged Indians and Pakistanis to a larger extent.

Indigenously the Indian work-force in middle east originated from Kerala, Maharashtra, Gujarat, Karnataka, Goa and Andhra Pradesh, Gulati (1983) found that 135000 Keralites by the end of 1977 were in the middle east. This went upto 137000 by 1979 when the total indians in middle east were 350000. This accounted for more than one half Indian work-force comprised of Keralited. By the early 1983's Keralites swelled to 300000 in the middle east making one third to the total Indian workers.

The outflow of well educated and working age-group personnel shall witnessed its impact on the region in particular. Lack of complete information and data makes these statements handicapped. By the year 1975 the migration of work force to middle east initiated a strong flow, however it witnessed relief of less than one per cent in all the Asian sending countries. By 1981 Pakistan and Philippines sent above 2% of their economically active population. In the case of India during 1981 comprised the highest majority to a tune of one million workers, but the relief of employment is only 0.4%.

A study of ILO's Asian Regional Team for Employment Promotion (ARTEP) on the impact of return migration on employment in Pakistan found three-quarter million families by the end of 1980 returned. Their re-absorption into previous jobs created adverse consequence on the economy. Wages have risen considerably than productivity, creating inflationary pressures on the economy. Secondly, the capital intensive technology owing to skills of the migrants, limited remittances have gone into the productive investments, rather construction and other tertiary occupations created a structural change in the economic set up. What is required is labour intensive projects, community developmental plans for women and children, organised in and out migration. Lastly the third dimension of which is the outcome of Government and Private sector combined to project out to study, investigate, survey analyse pilot projects to test and execute short and long term strategies in collaboration preferably with other countries. A mutual exchange programme would also go a long way in benefiting the returned migrants.

Although, large scale migration is apparent from the various Asian countries, yet the employment relief was negligible. The number of people migrated to middle east is not a really big number, but the remittances received has to some extent provided relief in the balance of payment and the country's economies in several. This was possible due to heavy remittances. However, the other side of the tragedy was the misuse of financial resources, lack of banking knowledge, insecurity or fear of investment, both in banks or in productive endeavours. Hence, in general, migrant workers were never been guided, directed encuraged to conserve their financial resources formally.

The ILO year book (1981) has shown during the year 1981, India had 266824000 economically active population, million were in the middle east. The overall employment relief was only 0.37 per cent. Pakistan had 24120000 economically active population 650000 were in the middle east and the relief calculated to 2.69 per cent. This figure is the highest amongst the Asian countries. The other country to have similar employment relief of 2.08 per cent is the Philippines, 0.92 per cent is reported from Korea. Thailand and Bangla Desh by 1981 had employment relief of 0.92 and 0.27 per cent respectively. [ILO, Nazil Choncri (1983), Sirajeldin (1983)].

The contract labour migration shall be continued inter-regionally and intra-regionally, particularly with change in skills. The labour importing countries are posing different new issues in which they are dominating skilled and professional labour. Apparently there appears to be slow migration from the labour exporting countries, but it is a steady feast, particularly the middle eastern countries have established a certain reliance on the migrant labour, that these exist certain attractive positions and fairly good income which is certainly highest than can be expected in the home country.

In Pakistan during the Fifth Five Year Plan (1978—83), one-third of the increase of its fast growing labour force found employment in the middle east. In case of India there was a little impact all over the country with the exception of Kerala state and partially, in the city of Hyderabad.

The annual Indian outflow of contract migrant workers to middle east show a slow trend from 1976 upto 1980. During the year 1976 only 42000 migrated to middle east. In the two years 1980 and 1981 about 268,200 and 272,000 contract migrants left India. After this peak, the trend is slowed down. The figures for the next two years viz. 1982 & 1983 were 224257 and 217971. For these two years the percentage of migrant workers to the middle east out of the total migrant to all countries of the world is given as 93.6 per cent and 96.9 per cent. Subsequently, the Indian labour to middle east showed down from 1984 onwards. The Annual outflow between 1984 to 87 in the respective years shows 198520 (94.6), 160396 (98.4), 109234 (96.1), 121812 (97.2). Rashid Amjad (1989). The conspicuous point is that the percentage share of migrants (given in parenthesis) has stayed above 95 per cent. Hence, the migration favour of the Indians for more than a decade and half remained the middle east and shall be remained for another decade presumably.

The remittances sent by the middle east migrant workers to India have shown a brighter side.

Indians remittances were 303 million US Dollars in the year 1977. At once it want up to 1542 US million dollars in the year 1981 and 1224 US million dollars in 1982. These higher remittances are the positive impact of high migration of flow of the workers. At the beginning of the migration the workers tend to remit on the higher side, eventually they restrict sending. However, they may keeps with themselves and get them at once to purchase a certain real estate during their visit to the home country. They realise that the receivers at home would misuse the money hence, they take a precautionary step.

The fifth coming year 1983 to 1985, India recorded remittances as 1418, 1451 and 1442 US million dollars respectively. The continued higher side of remittances and lesser number of migrants proceeding to Gulf explains that the already staying workers and the new ones together are remitting large amounts to India. (Rashid Amjad, 1989).

Tan (1987) showed that the skill mix of the migrant sending Indian workers to middle east during the year 1985 as 5.2 per cent professionals, 47.0 per cent skilled and semi-skilled, 40.1 per cent unskilled and 7.7 per cent others. This shows significantly, the unskilled labour yet has a brighter chance of migration. A very limited professionals and others have moved from India.

Tan (1987) also has shown in the year 1985-86, Philippines sent the highest professionals 15.1 per cent to the middle east. The skilled and semi-skilled categories is dominated by Pakistanis

52 per cent. Above 50 per cent of the unskilled were drawn from Bangla Desh and Sri Lanka. Except Philippines 13.5 per cent seamen, no other country had their representation from south and south-east Asia under this category.

REFERENCES

Ahmad Mansoor (1982), "Emigration of Scare skills in Pakistan, ILO, International Migration for Employment", Working Paper No. 5, Geneva.

Akbar Mahamood (1981), "Pakistan : Emigration for Employment", Report of ARPLA, Sympusium on overseas recruitment, ILO, Islamabad, May 1981.

Ali Syed Ashref et al. (1981), "Labour Migration from Bangla Desh to Middle East", World Bank Staff Working Paper No. 454, Washington, D.C.

Birks J.S. and Sinclair C.A. (1980), "Arab Man Power : The crisis of development", St. Martina Press, New York.

Bohning W.R. (1984), "International Migration : Implications for development policies", in U.N. Department of International Economic and Social Affairs, population distribution, migration and development, pp.379-403.

Chakravarthi N.R. (1971), "The Indian Minorities in Burma: The rise and decline of the immigrants community", Oxford University Press, London.

Demery (1983), "Asian labour migration to the middle east", Paper presented in the conference - Asian labour migration to middle east - East-West centre, Honolulu, Sept. 1983.

Edita, Tan (1983), "Adjustment of the labour market to the Foreign outflow of skilled labour - The case of construction workers" Bangkok, ARPLA, 1983.

Ermisch J. (1983), "The political economy of demographic change causes and implications of population trends in Great Britain", Heineman, London.

Ghai D.S. and Y.P. Ghai (Eds) (1970), "Portraits of a Minority", Oxford University Press, London.

Gilani, I. Jar, Khan K.F. and Iqbal M. (1981), "Labour migration from Pakistan to middle East and its impact on the domestic economy", Research Report Series, Islamabad.

Gulati Leela (1983), "Impacts of Male Migration to the Middle East on the Family: Some evidence from Kerala", Economic and Political Weekly, Bombay, No. 52, December 1983.

Jain P.C. (1982), "Indians abroad : A current populations estimate", Economic and Political Weekly, 20-Feb, pp. 299-304.

Keeley Charles (1980), "Asian workers migration to middle east", Working Paper No. 52, Centre for Policy Studies, The Population Council, New York.

Kim, Suyoria (1982), "Contract migration in the Republic of Korea", International Migration for Employment, Working Paper No. 4, ILO, Geneva, 1982.

Kondapi L. (1951), "Indians Overseas" (1838-1949), Oxford University Press, Madras.

Madhevan M.C. (1985), "Indian Emigrants, Numbers, Characteristics, and Economic Impact", Popualtion and Development Review, Vol. II, No. 3, September 1985, pp. 457-481.

Manlo I Abella (1984), "Labour migration from South and South East Asia : Some policy issues", International Labour Review, Vol. 123, No. 4, July-August, 1984.

Mathew S.J. (1983), "Letter from Kerala", For Eastern Economic Review, January 27, 1983.

Nair P.R. Gopinathan (1983), "Asian emigration to the middle east : Emigration from India", Trivandrum Centre for Development Studies, Working Paper No. 180.

Nanjundan S. (1950), "Indians in Malayan Economy", Office of Registrar, Government of India, New Delhi.

Omvedt G. (1980), "Migration in colonial India : The articulation of feudalism and capitalism by the colonial state", The Journal of Peasant Studies, 6, No. 2.

Rashid Amjad (1987), "To the Gulf and Beach", Studies on the economic impact on Asian Labour Migration - ILO, (ARTEP - Asian Regional Team for Employment Promotion), edited, New Delhi.

Rizwanul Islam (1981), "Export of manpower from Bangla Desh to middle eastern countries - The impact of remittances money on the household expenditure - NFRHRD, Dhaka".

Sandhu K.S. (1969), "Indians in Malaya : Some aspects of their immigration and settlement", 1786-1957, London, Cambridge University Press.

Shaheed, Farida (1981), "Migration and effects on women in the villages", Seminar - Rural Development of Women, Mahabaleshwar, India.

Siddiqi A.M.A.H. (1983), "Economic and Non-economic impact of migration from Bangladesh - An overview", Dhaka Manpower Planning Centre.

Sirajeldin (1983), "I and others, Manpower and international migration in the middle east and north Africa", A World Bank Publication, Oxford University Press.

Stabl, Charles W. (1981), "Contract labour migration from phillipines, Trends and Issues" Conference on International Migration in the Arab World, May 11-16, Nicosia, Cyprus, 1981.

Tan, Edita (1987), "Migration savings, remittances and labour supply behaviour - a comparative experience of Asian countries", ILO (ARTEP), New Delhi.

Tinker H. (1977), "The Banyan Tree : The overseas Immigrants from India, Pakistan and Bangla Desh", Oxford, Oxford University Press.

Weiner, Myrun (1982), "International Migration and Development : Indians in the Persian Gulf", Population and Development Review, March 1982.

3
SOCIAL CHARACTERISTICS RELATED TO THE HYDERABADI WORKERS REPATRIATED FROM KUWAIT

The social factors related to the human migration have a certain consequences on the decision-making. It is observed that the social characteristics like the age, sex, education, marital status, family status, religion, duration of stay become significant.

Education of the migrant plays a vital role in acquiring a job, which in turn reflects on the income. However, migration to work or higher education makes a difference. Particularly migration to work as in this study, had a mixed impact. In some professional cases education played a dominant role, still in some others the highly educated earned less than the less educated. Better jobs were held by the less educated ones.

The martial status also had its impact on the migration decision process. The young ones ventured to migrate first consolidate their economic position and go for a better bride. Those who were married long were hesitant to leave their wife and children alone. There were occasions of getting the family to the host country at the cost of high expenditure and low savings such a situation remained a temporary phenomena. Since, the cost of maintaining family at Kuwait was on a very higher side.

Religions ethos, sentimental attachments, psychological readiness were yet a few social stigmas associated with migration. An individual, a family and a community of migrates have a different approach towards migration. In the case of migration to the Gulf, one.

Community particularly the muslims were favoured than others. Hence, it can be safe to predict that religion also has a certain impact on the process of migration.

Duration of Stay (Period of Residence in Kuwait)

Temporal factor in geography is a widely used concept by the geographers to measure the magnitude of occurred transformation, both in terms of population and space. Longer duration of stay of the emigrants is associated with political, social, economic and cultural stability and security at the destination.

The duration of stay of the Hyderabadi population in Kuwait was related to better wages housing and working conditions. Freedom of religious practice, cultural heterogeneity and political non-interference.

The duration of residence of the Hyderabadis in Kuwait vis-a-vis Indians and all other immigrants in Kuwait from other countries of the world is given in Table 3.1.

Table 3.1

Classification by period of stay Hyderabadis in Kuwait

	< 5 yrs	*5-9*	*10-14*	*> 15 yrs*	*Total*
Hyderabadis	16.1	38.4	34.8	10.8	100
Indian	27.4	26.2	21.4	25.0	100
All immigrants labour from other countries of the world (1980 census) including Indians	45.0	23.0	16.0	16.0	100

Source : Survey, 1980 census of Kuwait referred in "Immigrant labour in Kuwait" by Al-Moosa 1985.

Duration of stay of Hyderabadis in Kuwait show by August 2nd 1990, when Iraq invaded Kuwait, about 10.8 per cent stayed for over 15 years, and only 16.1 per cent stayed for a minimum of less than 5 years. The major chunk of the migrant labour stayed between 5 to 15 years (72.2%) in Kuwait. The immigrant labour in Kuwait from all over the world by 1985 shows 16 per cent lived for over 15 years

(Indian 25% and Hyderabadis 10.8%). A majority of 45 per cent of the labour stayed below 5 years (Indians 27.4% and Hyderabadis 16.1%). These figures indicate that the Indians in Kuwait had a longer duration of residence and a majority of the other immigrant labour of the world has started to stabilise.

The Survey analysis of the occupational category-wise duration of stay of the Kuwaiti repatriates of Hyderabad is shown in the Table 3.2. Technicians and professionals have stayed beyond twenty-five years in Kuwait. The professionals include Engineers, Architects, Doctors, Computer analysts etc. Fifty-five per cent of the professionals, forty-seven per cent of the technicians, sixty per cent service persons engaged in and twenty three per cent of the drivers stayed for above ten years in Kuwait. The low percentage of the drivers stayed beyond ten years denotes that the demand for the Indian drivers in Kuwait is a recent phenomenon. Most of the Government departments recruited a large number of drivers from Hyderabad.

Table 3.2

Period of stay in Kuwait (Category-wise)

Period of years	*Profess-ionals*	*Techni-cals*	*Service and others*	*Drivers*	*Total*
1-2			6.6	6.7	3.5
2-5	18.2	3.3	10.0	20.0	12.5
5-8	13.6	26.7	13.3	13.3	17.0
10-15	40.9	33.3	50.0	16.7	34.8
15-25	9.1	6.7	10.0	6.7	8.1
< 25	4.6	6.7	-	-	2.7
Total	100	100	100	100	100

Source : Sample Survey Hyderabad - 1991.

Kuwait became saturated with migrants ten years back by 1980s, the lower and declining number of technicians, service drivers during the past ten years is evident. But the professionals were/are still in demand particularly Doctors, Engineers and computer analysts and allied category personnel.

During the past five years twenty per cent of the professionals and drivers have moved to Kuwait, ten per cent of the technicians left Hyderabad for Kuwait. This leaves an impression that the demand of technicians has reached the stage of saturation, because of the completion of the building activities and the country is fully developed and attracts only very high level personnel with sophistication and specialisation in all fields of development.

Amongst the personnel lived in Kuwait between 5-9 years, shows Hyderabadis (38.4%) were the maximum compared to that of Indians (26.2%) and all other immigrant labour (23.0%). Yet the stay of Hyderabadis between 10-14 years also shows a substantial percentage (34.8%) compared to Indians (21.4%) and other (16.0%). Hence it is observed that the people of Hyderabad made a strong base in Kuwait. A rough estimate uttered by the repatriates puts it to 6 to 7 thousand people of Hyderabadi origin lived prior to war in Kuwait.

Al-Moosa (1985) observed on the period of residence in Kuwait is a basic indicator of immigrant problem and it also reflects on satisfaction and stability, besides laws and regulations of the country. The immigrants, period of residence is also subject to the approval of his Kuwaiti sponsor kafeel, who need to recommend each time the permit expires. This depends on the immigrants production efficiency, loyalty, obedience and sponserers satisfaction.

"The House Lease Law" in Kuwait allow the owners to increase property rents by up to 100 per cent every five years. This law determined the period of residence for immigrant manpower, particularly those of the lower income group who pay direct rent on housing. If the wages earned and after the rent paid does not save sufficient money the immigrants are left with no choice except to leave the country. This particularly has no impact on the immigrants having government houses and the company quarters.

The other factors affecting the period of residence in Kuwait is related with the state budget. In 1982 with the falling in the oil resources, Kuwait suffered a deficit on KD 800 million, this and the residence law of 1982 evacuated 30,000 labourers having failed to obtain sponsorship (Kuwait, Daily News, 1982).

Residence in Kuwait is also connected with the immigrants social status, high placed professionals, physicians, accountants working under contract and which entitle them to return home once in a year tend to stay a longer duration than those who travel on their own expenses. Besides workers accompanied with their families and children intend to stay over a longer period. This is due to childrens education, and at the expense of lower rate of saving.

The immigrant labour stay in Kuwait vis-a-vis to their standard of education is derived by Al-Moosa. His survey has shown the least literates had a longer stay in Kuwait. Beyond seventy per cent of the labour possessing below secondary standard of education and the illiterates 64 per cent of them stayed over 15 years. Only 27.8 per cent of the graduates and 53.8 per cent of those who studied below university appeared to be living for over one and half decades in Kuwait (See Table 3.3).

Table 3.3

Immigrant labour in Kuwait - Standard of education by length of study in years

	Less than 5 yrs.	*5-9 yrs.*	*10-14 yrs*	*15 and above yrs.*
Illiterate	20.0	8.0	8.0	64.0
Read and Write	7.7	6.8	11.7	73.9
Below Secondary	6.3	10.2	12.1	71.4
Below University	11.6	17.5	17.1	53.8
Graduates	25.2	29.2	17.7	27.8
Total	14.9	18.0	15.0	52.0

Source : Sample Survey - 1981 - Al-moosa.

The immigrant labour which lived in Kuwait between 5-14 years were 16 per cent illiterates. 18.5 per cent could read and write 22.3 per cent below secondary, 34.6 per cent below university, 46.9% were graduates (Al-Moosa, 1985).

It is also found, those who entered into Kuwait in the late 1970s, and who lived for less than 5 years were found to be 25.2 per cent graduates and 20 per cent illiterates and all the other with some education were found to be below 12 per cent. This shows that illiterates and the graduates in the recent past were capable of entering into Kuwait. The demand for manual labour on the one side and those highly educated on the other were attracted to Kuwait.

Hence the duration of stay and the standard of education had a reverse impact. The illiterates were found in maximum per cent in the category of below 5 years and above 15 years of stay. The graduates however maintained a steady percentage in all the duration of stay ranges given in Table 3.3.

Sex Structure

The Male-Female ratio of manpower is an important indicator of the socio-economic trend of the society. Participation of the women folk in the labour force is a characteristic of the migrant communities. Generally, male migration and stability of income, housing and social status is correlated with the incoming of family and children. It is also a known fact that literate families move early and help themselves to stability. The illiterates seldom move.

The Hyderabadis in Kuwait, particularly those who had a longer period of stay in the host country lived along with their wife and children. The muslim women of Hyderabadi, at least at the lower echelons of the professions and incomes is only subjected to home-living. Females are not encouraged and allowed to work outside to a larger extent in the Muslim families.

In Kuwait, participation of Kuwaiti women is not restricted from working. However, the low standard of education, determination, cultural restrictions and strong economic base discourages their active participation in the work-force. This obviously creates favourable conditions for the immigrant women with more job opportunities.

The sex structure of the immigrant labour force in Kuwait under various occupational categories is shown in Table 3.4 Al-moosa (1985) derived from his Survey analysis (1981) seven occupational categories of work. The females (56.4%) dominated the white color jobs viz. scientific and technical than the males (38.1%) once again the female predomination is evident in clerical (21.3%) the male (16.5%) and service activities (21.6%) the male (6.2%). The overall labour force in Kuwait shows the highest (41.2%) in Scientific and Technical activities signifying that the country is advancing and developing in the fields of scientific and technical know how. Production and labour activities (20.0%) and clerical (17.3%) are the

Table 3.4

Sex by Occupation : All immigrant labour in Kuwait

	Scientific and Technical	*Administrative and Management*	*Clerical and Executive*	*Sales*	*Services*	*Agriculture and Fisheries*	*Production and Labour*	*Total*
Male	38.1	4.8	16.5	9.8	6.2	0.7	23.9	100
Female	58.4	0.7	21.3	0.3	20.6	-	0.7	100
Total	41.2	4.1	17.3	8.2	8.6	0.6	20.0	100

Source : Sample Survey (1981) Al-moosa.

other major fields of occupations. The female participation is nill in agriculture and fishing, negligible in sales (0.3%) administrative and managerial categories (0.7%).

Women in India are found in all forms of economic activities. The rural India, has the highest women folk engaged in primary activities. The urban women is found in all forms of tertiary activities. The very low participation of women in production, sales, administration and management is contrary to the Indian conditions.

The survey analysis of the Hyderabadi female in Kuwait and their occupational structure is given in Table 3.5.

Table 3.5

Participation of Hyderabadi women in working force in Kuwait 1991

Professionals	10 per cent
Technicians	30 per cent
Service and other allied activities	60 per cent
Total	100 per cent

Source : Sample Survey Hyderabad—1991

It is observed from the Table 3.5 that the female folk of the Hyderabad ventured to participate, sixty per cent of them in service and other activities. This constituted, basically, teaching, tailoring, household jobs and a few ministerial assignments. The thirty per cent of women in technical fields is exclusively in paramedical and computers, besides a few of them were employed as translators of foreign languages. The professionals, once again are the computer analysts and doctors.

The Survey results of the comparative analysis of the male-female participation under the various broad fields of occupation of the Kuwaiti repatriates of Hyderabad is given in Table 3.6.

It is seen from the Table 3.6 the male constituted 95.5 per cent of professionals and 4.5 per cent of females, ninety per cent were male technicians and ten per cent female, the service category comprised of 80 per cent male and 20 per cent females. The overall, picture shows, around 9 per cent of Hyderabadi women were actively participating in the work-force.

Table 3.6

Sex of the migrant occupation-wise

	Professionals	*Technicals*	*Service and others*	*Drivers*	*Total*
Male	95.5	90.0	80.0	100	91.1
Female	4.5	10.0	20.0	-	8.9
Total	100	100	100	100	100

Source : Sample Survey (1981)—Al-moosa.

Al-moosa (1985) found in his sample survey 82.8 per cent sales and 17.2 per cent females were in the immigrant labour force of Kuwait in the year 1981. The Hyderabadis in the sample survey showed 91 per cent of male and 9 per cent of female participated in the labour force during their stay in Kuwait. He also observed that the sex structure of the immigrant labour force in Kuwait is related to the age structure. Females are concentrated in the younger categories and males in the older categories. He observed females dominated in the category of under 30 age group and the males in over 50 age group.

It is also found in Kuwait, sex structure shows less relation to educational standards. The female have received a good schooling than the males, the female with higher educational standard obtained easy access up to scientific and technical occupations, including teaching. The male counter parts with lower educational background and willingness to accept manual jobs, find themselves in occupations where the interview is not tougher. They are willing to work hard and overtime to earn extra wages and send them to their home countries.

In the case of Hyderabadi women also the same facts are revealed during the interview and survey analysis. It is found that the females of Hyderabad were educated in good schools and obtained a preliminary technology in computers and para-medical courses and also in the teaching professions before leaving to work in Kuwait.

Age Structure

Aging is one of the social indicator in the demographic analysis. Generally, age and sex ratio pyramids are drawn to elicit relationship between the two variables. However, age structure of a given community society has much to do with the developmental activities. Planners take up active consideration to study the existing and expected age-groups which contributes in the economic development. A country bestowed with higher ratio of working population (Age-group 18-60 years) guarantees a potential working labour.

Age structure and Migration has much in correlation. The young male working age groups always venture overseas. Although Ravenstein states females are more migratory than males is mostly confined to within the region, but the male population are always in search of better opportunities abroad and they venture long distances is in acceptance to his law. However children and the age-old population are not attracted towards migration. They tend to stabilize and satisfy themselves within their home country. However, youth attaining working age always service to migrate.

The migration from the city of Hyderabad to Kuwait, has also witnessed, that the younger ones are always willing to go anywhere in to South West Asian countries. However, it is also a fact that a large majority of the Hyderabadis ventured to go abroad irrespective of age. This is mainly attributed to the fact that these countries were attracting people with experience and with high pay packages, better working conditions, free annual or bi-annual home trips.

Hyderabad, experienced all age-groups to migrate, the Muslim community in particular for reasons of employment, religion and economic stability always thronged to an opportune suitable to their satisfaction. The Keralites from India are the first, irrespective of age-groups who migrated and are still willing to do so to the countries of South-West Asia.

The elderly age-group, when substantiated their position in the Gulf arranged for a visa and a job for their children. They themselves staying for a couple of years came back to Hyderabad to direct their savings in a better and productive means of assets and livelihood consolidating their economic standards.

The foreign labour force by age group in Kuwait Moosa (1985) and the Indians (including Hyderabadis in Kuwait) and the Hyderabadis (Survey analysis, 1991) is given in Table 3.7.

Al-moosa in his survey analysis of the immigrant labour force in Kuwait recorded 72 per cent in the age groups of 20-39 years, the Kuwait census has shown the Indian constituted under this age group to only 10.2 per cent. However, the survey made in Hyderabad (1991) has shown 39.3 per cent represented to be the labour below 40 years of age. The age-group of 40-60 years and above is shown by Moosa as 28 per cent, the Kuwaiti census has shown below 15 per cent and the survey in Hyderabad accounted for more than 60 per cent of Hyderabadis constituted in this age-groups. Once again it is confirmed that the people from Hyderabad irrespective of age and job security ventured to go overseas as the opportunity of earning and saving were more.

Table 3.7

The foreign labour force by age group

Age group	*All immigrant labour in Kuwait*	*Hyderabadis in Kuwait*	*Indians in Kuwait (incl. Hyderabadis)*
20-29	38.4	6.3	5.3
30-39	33.7	33.0	4.9
40-49	19.7	37.5	4.9
50-59	6.8	21.4	4.9
60 and over	1.4	1.8	4.9
Total	100	100	5.0

Source : Sample Survey 1981 - Al-moosa.

Kuwait Annual Statistical Abstract, 1982 (Table 84) Sample Survey, 1990.

The foreign labour force in Kuwait by sex and by age group is calculated by Al-moosa for all the immigrant labour force and the Hyderabadis is extracted from the sample survey (1991). See Table 3.8.

The labour force below 29 years of age totalled to 18.8 per cent for all the immigrants in Kuwait, but Hyderabadis represented only

6.3 per cent. However, the female components of 38.6 per cent and 45.8 per cent of all immigrants and Hyderabadis respectively confirms the fact that the female below 29 years reached Kuwait either by marriage or along with their parents or with a contract job. The highest (45.8%) figure of the females of Hyderabadis origin in Kuwait also suggests that Kuwait has more freedom and security to women along with better perks and working conditions as against any other country of the Gulf. The fact also applies to the other female immigrants from different countries of the world to Kuwait.

Table 3.8

Foreign labour force : Sex by age group

		< 29 yrs	*30-39*	*40-49*	*50 & over*	*Total*
Hyderabadis	Male	13.2	42.3	28.7	15.8	91.1
in Kuwait	Female	45.8	33.7	15.1	5.4	8.9
	Total	6.3	33.0	37.5	23.2	100
All	Male	14.7	33.9	34.8	16.6	82.8
immigrants	Female	38.6	41.0	16.0	3.8	17.2
in Kuwait	Total	18.8	35.1	31.7	14.4	100

Source : Sample Survey - 1991, Hyderabad and Sample Survey - Al-moosa - 1981, Kuwait.

The low values of the male labour force (14.7%) and (13.2%) for all immigrants and Hyderabadis presents a view that under this age group the female migrate in excess to that of the young male labour. The labour force in the age-groups of 30-39 years shows 35.1 per cent and 33.0 per cent respectively for all immigrant labour and Hyderabadi labour force in Kuwait. The male and female labour is in close proximity to the total percentage under this age-group, the total male immigrant labour force was 33.9 per cent as against 42.3 per cent of the Hyderabadi male labour. The female, total immigrant labour was 41.0 per cent and the Hyderabadis female labour accounted for 33.7 per cent.

The male and female labour force of Hyderabad in Kuwait in the age-group of 30-39 years shows the stable families, who have well settled along with their children in Kuwait. This age group appears to be, both male and female are actively participating in economic activities. However, a slight increase of males can be attributed to the fact that they cannot get their families due to their low earnings. Housing, children's education and other reasons.

The table also shows a high total for the age-groups of 40-49 years. The conspicuous excess male figures of all migrants (34.8%) and low values of the Hyderabadi labour (28.7%) foretells that the latter start return migration for the sake of rehabilitation in the home-country. All those in possession of permanent stable and pensionable government jobs prefer to comeback and join their old service. They feel that it is safer to stay back and invest their savings in a productive manner, care for their growing children, construction/renovation of houses and so on.

The percentage calculated has shown with the increase of age regularly there is a fall of the male labour. The female labour also comes down as their age increases. This is due to the fact that they would prefer to settle down with their children in Hyderabad and plan for their future. The male returnees may delay coming but prefer to send away the family to Hyderabad so as to establish and rehabilitate themselves with the already accumulated assets and savings at their home town.

Age Composition/Structure of Hyderabadi Workers in Kuwait

Working age of population is the potential stage of putting extra effort and energy for newer and challenging pursuits. Viability and utility of the workers age destines to establish the socio-economic basis of any individual. Age is dynamic in nature, experience and age of the workers are more parallel to achieve new ideas, change of views, satisfactory decision-making is challenged by the workers age and experience.

Age in the process of mobility, selection of work has a significant role. Mobility of workers from one place to another, duration of stay in a particular place and establishment, the factor of the age plays a vital role, younger workers are more in demand. The challenges of the job are well satisfied by the younger generation in terms of their potentiality, ability and skill.

The survey has shown as much as seventy per cent of the migrant workers were in the age group of thirty to fifty years.

Migration demands more potential age group. The young workers below thirty years are the least. Between fifty to sixty years of age group worker constituted about twenty per cent of the migrants.

Professionals, servicians and drivers constitutes seventy per cent in the age group of thirty to fifty years. Eighty per cent of the technicians fall under this group. The technician skill requires energetic workers below fifty years to carry out the job satisfactorily.

Work force in the age group below thirty years are a few service and professionals. None of the technicians and drivers belonged to this group. Insignificant number of professionals and technicians are found in above sixty years age group. Hence, it is concluded that the composition and demand of the workers is in the age group of thirty to fifty years.

The middle aged migrated people, either were invited by their relatives or deputed by the companies/government. This assures their job security/guaranteed in India. But finding the comfortable social life and better economic position such people have made sure to settle their sons/daughters/brothers by arranging a visa in the host country and if the situation so-called then only they come back to Hyderabad to join bach in the old service. Hence all types of age-groups have utilized the present economic boom to west Asia. Particularly the persian Gulf, Saudi Arabia were the most attracted places for the Muslims all over the world and for Hyderabadi muslims is not an exception.

The repatriated Hyderabadi labour from Kuwait, by occupation and age-group is depicted in Table 3.9.

The age group of 25-29 years has shown that only 6.3 per cent of Hyderabadis lived in Kuwait of this age-group. There were neither technicians nor drivers below 29 years of age. The service sector had 16.7 per cent and 9.1 per cent of the professionals resided in Kuwait in the abovementioned age-group.

In the age-group of 30-49 years seventy per cent of the Hyderabadi labour lived in Kuwait. It comprised of 69.2%, 83.3%, 63.3% and 66.7% of the professionals, technicians, service and drivers respectively. This is a very potential and productive age group, hereafter the trend is changed.

Table 3.9

Hyderabadi labour in Kuwait by occupation and age group

Age in years	*Profess-ionals*	*Techni-cals*	*Service and others*	*Drivers*	*Total*
25-29	9.1	-	16.7	-	6.3
30-39	36.4	43.3	23.3	30.0	33.0
40-49	31.8	40.0	40.0	36.7	37.5
50-59	18.2	13.3	20.0	33.7	21.4
> 60	4.5	3.4	-	-	1.8
Total	100.0	100.0	100.0	100.0	100.0

Source : Sample Survey - 1991 - Hyderabad.

The labour force in the age-group of 50 to above 60 years of age show 23.2 per cent stayed in Kuwait. A majority of 33.7 per cent of the drivers were conspicuous under this age group, 20 per cent are in the service sector. The professionals comprised of 22.7 per cent and only 16.7 per cent the technicians are found in this age-group.

Finally, it is observed that, Kuwait had a substantial of its immigrant labour force in the productive age-groups. It is also evident, that the labour percentage started to decline for above 50 years of age. As already pointed out this is due to the immigrants speculative plans to get back to their home countries to join their past profession, construction, of own houses and other productive activities.

The Hyderabadi labour particularly, the muslim youth, with their higher responsibilities, dearth of employment opportunities claiming to the attractive offers in Kuwait. The middle-aged ones, due to their experience were in demand and, however, not many with 50 years and above age seriously planned to emigrate from Hyderabad.

Religious Composition of Hyderabadi Labour in Kuwait

The City of Hyderabad has a composite culture, it has originated though a blend of many religious, customs, brotherhood friendship and respect for every religion and tradition. Hyderabad in the Indian cities emerged as a unique centre of cultural and religious ethos. As it was ruled upto 1948 by Muslim kings, the Nizam's before getting merged with the Indian union. Hence, to a certain extent, the impact of language, tradition, culture and character of Islam is prevalent and predominate.

Religion

The sample survey has also undertaken the share of the religion of the migrant to highlight the attraction of various religious groups among migrants. Kuwait a muslim monarchs country has adopted a liberal policy in terms of the appointment of the people with different religion. Kuwait has attracted and encouraged the largest non-muslim crowd among the Gulf countries.

The distribution of muslims and non-muslims occupation-wise migrated to Kuwait shows eighty-six per cent were muslims and fourteen per cent non-muslims. Ninety per cent of the muslims were working as professionals and drivers. The non-muslims had their greatest representation as technicians followed by service, drivers and professionals. Dominantly, the non-muslim women technicians were in the paramedical staff, men were mechanics, welders, turners, dentors, sales representatives, and so on. A large number of non-muslim were among the drivers category. Few were engineers and computer technicians and professionals. It is clear from the following table the share of muslims and non-muslims in the various categories of occupation (see Table 3.10).

Table 3.10

Religious composition of the Hyderabadi labour in Kuwait by occupation-wise

Religion	*Profess-ionals*	*Techni-cals*	*Service and others*	*Drivers*	*Total*
Muslims	90.1	80.0	83.3	90.0	85.7
Non-muslims	9.1	20.0	16.7	10.0	14.3
Total	100.0	100.0	100.0	100.0	100.0

Source : Sample Survey - 1991 - Hyderabad.

Kuwait, had never been a strong Islamic state alone, it is liberal with all religious. There were a few churches and temples scattered. In Bahrain there is one Balakrishna temple located in Souk, which is more then 100 years old. The Sultan of Oman allowed to build a Hindu temple near the palace compound in Muscat, however the south-west Asian countries restrict free religious ordeals for the non-muslims, hence religions is a private personnel issue.

Residential Family Status

The following is the analysis of the various workers who afforded to migrate and stayed with their families and children in Kuwait. The work-force who had various concessions like free family accommodation, car and other benefits related to their jobs remained long with their families. Others includes those who were drawing salaries above KD 400 (Kuwaiti Dinar) per month had the right to invite their families and were also capable of maintaining the expenditure required to survive alongwith the family.

The prime objective of the migrants was to accumulate wealth and finally settled down in home town. Consistent uninterrupted and smooth stay for longer period made the workers to be attached to their families in Kuwait, however they did not loose their socio-cultural ties with their native city and country. Large real estates, shares, debentures were purchased by these migrants and were pretty sure that after their return they shall be accomplished with a guaranteed luxurious and better economic life (see Table 3.11).

Table 3.11

Hyderabadi workers in Kuwaiti Family Status - (Occupation-wise) per cent

	Profess-ionals	*Techni-cals*	*Service and others*	*Drivers*	*Total*
Resided with family	90.9	46.7	40.0	-	41.1
Resided alone	9.1	53.3	60.0	100.0	58.9
Total	100.0	100.0	100.0	100.0	100.0

Source : Sample Survey - 1991 - Hyderabad.

The Table 3.11 denotes about sixty per cent of the workers were leading lonely life and forty per cent of them have stayed along with their families. Ninety per cent of the professionals, forty-seven per cent technicians and forty per cent servicians lived with their families. Hundred per cent of the drivers stayed without families. This is due to low income and the type of job involved, the amount of salary/wages do not allow these people to stay with families. None of the free concessions to settle with families guarantee their employment.

It was already mentioned that staying alone or staying with family is related to the amount of income per month, facilities like cheaper accommodation, education to the children security of the female members and above all the heavy expenditure discourages staying with family. Generally newly married couples venture to stay together. This is a regular phenomenon in the city of Hyderabad that whoever gets newly married invites his wife at least on a visiting visa and attempts to retain her back. It is not possible then he would send her back with lots of gold, sarees, money etc. by promising that he would call her back at the earliest.

Al-moosa (1985) found in his survey of immigrant labour in Kuwait that the workers accompanied by their wives and children remain for longer periods. The immigration of the whole family indicates their intention to stay longer as the children will go to school. Also the presence of the whole family in Kuwait means greater expenses and a lower rate of saving so the family will be compelled to stay for a longer period to achieve maximum savings, a factor which explains why 52 per cent of the sample house-holds have been in Kuwait 15 years and more.

Hence, it has become clear that the workers longer duration of stay, job proficiency, high wages and permisibility of rules and laws of the state, lesser savings and high expenditure in Kuwait is associated to stay with families. However, when the women and children in the family take employment in Kuwait, the situation is different and eases the stay of the workers alongwith families. Hence educated wives generally obtain a certain job and prefer to accompany their husbands.

Marital Status

Intention to marry of the Hyderabadi workers in Kuwait is related to the employment security, income, adequate saving and so on. A separate survey may be necessary to analyse so as to how many of the young boys in Hyderabad were married to the sisters and daughters of those workers who are well settled overseas and that they guarantee a visa for them abroad in exchange of marriage.The Hyderabadi youth initially did not get attracted to such favours due to fear of getting socially demoraled. However, the poverty, unemployment and inability to procure a visa easily forced them to accept such proposals. Observation reveals that the young male members get exhausted attempting for a suitable job despite in possession of appropriate experience and qualifications. The overseas guarantee of a better employment and bright prospects tend to attract them to do anything to reach overseas. However, the after marriage repercussions on his own family members are not formidable.

The problem of the muslim females of marriageable age is wide. Girls who are well educated demand for equally or over qualified boys. This is generally not possible for the fact that most of the minority young boys are not interested in formal qualifications, they are interested in professional and technical training's which promise them a suitable job overseas. After they are successful of getting a job and return to their home town, they prefer marry a young and beautiful girl, not much qualified, and that they do not demand for dowry or any other conditions on marriage. The girls who do not have much qualification but are good looking, tall and young aged are most suitable and most wanted by the immigrant boys. Hence, the market of marriage is fluctuating, especially in the wake of the stream of migration to the Gulf. A variety of issues and problems have entered into the immigrant families of the Hyderabad. Lack of data and survey is the handicap to prolong this discussion.

Immigrant Labour in Kuwait—Sex by Marital Status

Al-moosa (1985) recorded in his survey the various marital status of the immigrant labour in Kuwait sex-wise.(see Table 3.12).

The survey has revealed 10.4 per cent lived single/bachelor, 85.0 per cent were married and were accompanied by spouses 3.1 per cent are married but un-accompanied by spouse and there were 0.5 per cent divorced and 0.9 per cent widows or widowers. The male-female constitution of marital status has emerged that there were 19 per cent female against 8.6 per cent males living single in Kuwait. The excess of female single workers are predominately engaged into paramedical services. It is seen 88.1 per cent of males are accompanied by their spouses. It was 70.0 per cent for the females. The married but unaccompanied by spouse, divorced or widowed have shown meager percentages. Hence, it is observed that most of the immigrant labour are living with their spouses in Kuwait.

Table 3.12

Immigrant labour in Kuwait - Sex by marital status

	Single	*Married accompanied by spouse*	*Married un-accompanied by spouse*	*Divorced*	*Widow/ Widower*
Male	8.6	88.1	3.1	0.1	0.1
Female	19.0	70.0	3.4	2.8	4.8
Total	10.4	85.0	3.1	0.5	0.9

Source: Sample survey - Al-Moosa 1981 - Immigrant Labour in Kuwait.

Marital Status of Hyderabadi Workers Before and After Migration to Kuwait

Pre and post marital status determines as one of the cause of the migratory decision-making process. Workers before marriage are the most challenging and endeavour to go to any country or any type of job/salary as their economic destination. Post marriage status creates complexities and leaves people undetermined and indecisive to venture migration.

Socio-economic conditions, family burden and responsibilities, stress, strain and security of job and maltreatments frustrates the individuals to migrate for a better economic destination. The encouragement and higher wages from the Gulf countries provide high satisfaction to both the married and unmarried workers to migrate.

The marital status of the workers before and after migration as shown in the Table 3.13 denotes that seventy per cent of the professionals sixty percent technicians and about fifty-seven per cent service people were unmarried before migration. But cent percent of the drivers were married prior to their migration to Kuwait. This is due to delayed demand of labour in Kuwait. Furthermore the drivers who migrated to Kuwait were mostly employed in the Road Transport Corporation of the State in Hyderabad. At Kuwait they were mostly appointed by the various ministries. Hence the marriage criterion did not emerge as a stronger binding factor. The income limit and the type of transport service generally discourage the drivers for early marriage.

Table 3.13

Hyderabadi workers in Kuwait - Marital status (occupation-wise) (before & after migration)

	Before Migration			*After Migration*		
	Married	*Single*	*Divorced*	*Married*	*Single*	*Divorced*
Professionals	31.8	68.2	-	81.9	18.2	-
Technicians	40.0	60.0	-	90.0	3.3	6.7
Service & Others	43.3	56.7	-	60.0	40.0	-
Drivers	100.0	-	-	100.0	-	-

Source: Sample Survey - Hyderabad - 1991.

The post marital status after migration showed eighteen per cent professionals, three per cent technicians and forty per cent of the service group were unmarried. About seven per cent of the technicians were either divorced or separated from the marital bondage.

The table also indicates that twenty to thirty per cent of these who migrated were married after migration. It is this cream of the people who had celebrated in a grand style their marriage at a very heavy financial expenditure. However these people did not demand or force dowry for their marriage. This enabled the bridal side to spend more money in decorative ornamental and dinner expenditure from their side.

Among the muslim community of Hyderabad the girls beautiful looking tall and elegant were highly preferred. Educational background of the girl was least important for marriage, in fact higher education was a curse for a better bridegroom. The young bachelors basically with lesser education but better income hesitated to marry a girl more than their education for the fear of domination by the girl in taking decisions and also they felt that the girls in their absence would not stay back at their in laws house or they would venture for a job outside to spend their time. The fear physychosis made most of the parents either to lie about the educational background of the girl or it forced them to stop education of their female child.

However this phenomenon is predominant in the middle and lower classes. The upper middle and the higher strata welcomed the education of girls and many such marriages rather late marriages have been observed in the muslim society. It can also be generalized that the muslim society had enormous socio-cultural educational and economic transformation undergone between 1970 to 1990.

Immigrant Workers in Kuwait and their Educational Standard

The economic change and development of Kuwait since 1950s placed a deterrent demand on a better educated and better trained and experienced personnel. The position was made worse by the exponential growth of the intelligence population at rates thought to be among the highest in the world. For a long the population in Kuwait was in majority aged below 15 years. This aggravated a situation where along with education, the teaching faculty, infrastructure and the whole educational system needed to be imported and organised and revamped.

Kuwait provided free education for its expatriate community and for its own citizens. However, in the recent past it started to impose restrictions on free education. This was due to increase in the number of students and decrease of teachers. However, the university education is free to all students in Kuwait. The demand for education among the school children forced the Kuwait Government to run evening schools and entertain private schools under the supervision of the educational ministry of Kuwait. The privatisation of education created a certain problem of admission and administration however the standard of education remind high in private schools.

The children of the immigrant labour children preferred to join technical and scientific studies as against the Kuwaiti children who were interested to study art, culture and other theoretical studies. The Kuwaiti Government has however imposed restriction on technical education. By then it was the children of the immigrants who swelled the technical education list.

The Kuwait 1981-82 census statistics have shown that the majority of the immigrate students were found in scientific, technical and medical faculties and their representation was thinner in Arts, Law, Commerce and hence the Kuwaitis are present among the administrators and executive white collars, whereas the immigrants are in specialized professions, scientific and technical fields.

The immigrant students particularly the Palestinians are present in most of the schools and are meritorious, the Kuwaiti students do not appear in most of the public schools, besides their merit is also low in studies. This attitude could be the result of the feelings of both parents and students that they are the "lords lot" of Kuwait and they need not work hard. Given the guarantee of economic prosperity and future stability apparently, psychologically and socially they feel that education is not compulsory. This may have high negative feed back in the days to come.

Dearth of Kuwaiti teachers, large immigrant students, understanding of Arabic language at the beginning, socio-psychological crisis appears to discourage the Kuwaiti student, hence alienation. The Kuwaitis do not set interested in taking teaching profession, this is due to social status, low wages are a few reasons for the Kuwaiti citizens reluctant to accept the teacher posts.

It is observed that the illiterate immigrant labour of Kuwait totals to 28.9 per cent 36.4 per cent of Kuwaitis and 24.2 per cent of all immigrants, but only 0.9 per cent of the Hyderabadi workers in Kuwait were illiterate. The highest per cent of the Kuwaiti illiterate workers reflects on the weak educational attention on the natives and that the natives are paid excess salaries and guarantee of the better and easy availability of job in their home state. Hence, the native are reluctant to put extra energies on obtaining education.

About 19 per cent of the total immigrant labour force can only read and write with no formal education certificates. This category has 22.1 per cent of all immigrant labour force, 14.3 per cent Kuwaitis, more of the Hyderabadi workers. The Kuwait labour 21.7 per cent is in possession of primary school certificate, where as the non-Kuwaitis 16 per cent. The workers from Hyderabad 14.3 per cent survived in Kuwait with only primary education.

The middle school qualification as shown by the Kuwaiti census 1982 is 15.1 per cent, the Kuwaitis 16.2 percent and the non-Kuwaitis 14.7 per cent are closer to the state average. However, Hyderabadi workers 28.6 per cent are in possession of middle school certificate which is nearly double to the national average. This is also a second largest educational class of the Hyderabadi workers, the first and the highest majority of the workers were graduates 38.4 per cent.

The secondary and equivalent education, the graduates and above of the Kuwait and other immigrant labour percentage is low. The Hyderabadi workers were comparatively more educated than the Kuwaitis or that of all the immigrant labour in Kuwait. The 2.4 per cent of the Kuwaiti graduates and 38.4 per cent of the Hyderabadi is a proud figure indeed.

The Non-Kuwaiti and total graduates of the labour force is also very low, depicting the lower educational potential among all workers. The Hyderabadi graduates make a strong impact on the overall labour structure of Kuwait.

Comparative Educational Attainment of the Immigrant Labour Force in their Country of Origin, Kuwaitis and Hyderabadi Workers by Occupation

The educational attainment in their home countries of the immigrant labour and Hyderabadis and that of the Kuwaitis has been compared to assess the relationship between education and employment in Kuwait. The figures for immigrant labour and Kuwaitis is derived from the survey of Al-Moosa (1981) and the Hyderabadi workers in Kuwait by the sample survey at Hyderabad—1991 (See Table 3.14).

The education of the immigrant workers is obtained at their countries of origin. The emigration for work generally has nothing to do with acquiring education. Attempt here is made to study the typology of the personnel with various levels of education and the type of job acquired.

The illiterates are conspicuously not found in scientific, technical, administrative and management jobs. They are predominantly present in the production, labour and service sectors. The immigrant labour particularly the Non-Kuwaiti Arab illiterates are predominant in agriculture, fisheries, production labour and service. The Kuwaiti illiterates 58.7 per cent in services and 36.0 per cent in production

Table 3.14

Comparative educational attainment of immigrant labour in their country of origin and Hyderabadis by occupation

		Scientific & Technical	*Administrative & Management*	*Clerical & Executive*	*Sales*	*Services*	*Agriculture & Fisheries*	*Production & Labour*
Illiterate	1	-	-	4.6	4.6	22.8	38.7	29.5
	2	-	-	1.3	2.7	58.7	1.3	36.0
	3	-	-	-	-	0.9	-	20.0
Read & Write	1	3.2	-	5.8	9.1	12.3	29.9	39.6
	2	5.5	0.5	9.1	13.2	23.2	2.3	46.4
	3	-	-	-	-	-	-	-
Below Secondary	1	12.8	-	10.4	16.6	5.2	16.5	38.4
	2	12.8	2.1	16.8	15.7	10.2	1.0	41.4
	3	-	30.1	30.1	51.2	61.5	-	34.1

(Contd.)

		Scientific & Technical	*Administrative & Management*	*Clerical & Executive*	*Sales*	*Services*	*Agriculture & Fisheries*	*Production & Labour*
Below University	1	49.4	2.3	25.3	7.7	1.3	1.7	12.4
	2	41.1	4.8	34.1	8.5	0.6	-	10.8
	3	9.1	23.3	36.6	32.1	28.9	-	30.3
Graduates & above	1	79.2	8.8	8.5	2.3	0.8	-	0.5
	2	80.2	6.8	10.2	1.8	0.7	-	0.4
	3	90.9	46.6	13.3	16.7	8.7	-	5.6
Total	1	44.5	3.8	12.1	7.5	4.4	9.8	17.9
	2	41.2	4.1	17.3	8.2	8.6	0.6	20.0
	3	-	-	-	-	-	-	-

Source: Nos. 1 & 2 Al-Moosa—Sample Survey - 1981 No. 1 Immigrants
No. 3 Sample Survey Hyderabad—1991 No. 2 Kuwaitis
No. 3 Hyderabadis

and labour is a matter of concern to Kuwait. Since Kuwait remained one of the richest country in the world cannot see its citizens to stay illiterate and concentrate only in primary and secondary sectors. There is a strong necessity to upgrade the indigenous population in the sphere of education in Kuwait.

The workers from Hyderabad in Kuwait who are illiterates formed 20 per cent in the production and labour. These are the people who have migrated very long and stayed back under this category.

The immigrant labourers in Kuwait who can read and write, appeared in the production and labour sector, the Kuwaitis (46.4%) large number is once again is a matter of concern. The agricultural activities are dominated by Non-Kuwaiti Arab immigrants who entered Kuwait in the first phase of migration from the surrounding environs due to oil boom. None of the Hyderabadi workers were found in this category.

Secondary education provided employment in all sectors of economy. The scientific, technical, administration and management production and labour activities are captured by the workers who possessed just a level of secondary education. This implies Kuwaiti economy is more concerned about the execution and operation of work, rather than educational attainments irrespective of the natives or other nationals.

The workers from Hyderabad, except in agriculture and fisheries are predominantly found in all other categories of employment in a large percentage. The highest of 61.5 per cent in servicees and 51.2 per cent in sales and above 30 per cent in all the other categories, shows, that the workers (particularly Muslim minority population) who generally are dropouts at secondary level. The continuous efforts to migrate and willingness to join any occupation has shown their presence in majority all over the Gulf countries. A large number of the employees already working under scientific and administrate or service organisation, utilised their work experience to procure 'Visa'. Their educational limitations never restricted their choice of employment. hence, a large majority of the Hyderabadis with below secondary education and of course with appropriate experience were well-settled in Kuwait.

The workers who had their education below university level were predominant as clerks. It is seen 25.3 per cent immigrant workers 34.1 Kuwaitis and 36.6 per cent of the Hyderabadis were working as clerks. The next order of preference is the production and labour. This is due to availability of overtime and extra wages hence extra savings. Besides, the clerks in the day duty also take up illegal employment either evenings or nights either in sales, production and labour jobs. Since they are aliens in the host country, they do not hesitate to carry any hard work or menial job.

With certainty it cannot be roped with all immigrants to do multiple jobs. However, observation and revealings by the Hyderabadi workers ascertained to a certain degree that a single job in foreign country is only at the beginning stage. Once they return after one visit to their home country they search for some part-time occupation in addition to that of the regular. The motive is to earn more money in a lesser duration. Those who are single venture for part time than those with families.

The field of scientific and technical employment in Table 3.14 shows a higher immigrant and Kuwaiti workers percentage 49.4 & 41.1 per cent respectively. The Hyderabadis are only 9.1 per cent. This is a sector which has a policy implications. The Kuwaiti administration prefer to appoint Arabs and Kuwaitis in this sector irrespective of low standards of education but with high salary and perks benefits. However, Americans and Europeans also constitute in large numbers at the higher echelous of employment.

The graduate workers are in majority employed into scientific and technical employment. Above 80 per cent of immigrants, Kuwaitis and Hyderabadi graduates are working in this sector. As already pointed out, the personnel in this sector are highly paid, guaranteed longer duration of stay with family and children, free accommodation, health care, school education and transport facility.

The immigrant graduates probably are arabs, Americans, Europeans and Japanese. However 90 per cent of the Hyderabadi graduates taking professional employment, and 4.6 per cent administrative and management shows that education has direct impact to the employment in Kuwait. Hyderabadis combine experience with education, since this is the real basis to procure a white collar job in Kuwait. Both education and employment are complementary to employment.

Level of Education

Education is one of the dominant variable with regard to socio-economic selectivity of migration. However different studies have kept the variable in debate but suggest that the better educated have a wider choice and more propensity to migration acceptance. There is a correlation between education and socio-economic status which in turn links education with employment; and the latter linked with income and this again established the socio-economic status of the migrant.

Choice of selection of a job, change of a job with confidence is left with education. But in Kuwait the migration trend has shown that the least educated had the first opportunity to move and work as labourers in the construction activity and technician in the building activity. The second stream was that of the educated lot invited to maintain, administer and run the various project joints. Business, Banks, Education and Health sectors attracted more of skilled, semi-skilled and educated to some extent with training and experience to work.

The educational attainment of the migrants did not change before and after their migration. Basically people went to Gulf countries to serve and earn. There were none who went to pursue higher education or training to (the Kuwait, Gulf States). Hence there was no change in the level of education of the migrants. There is evidence to believe that some of the employees irrespective of their required qualifications did undertake certain jobs of excellence. Particularly in the field of Engineering and Architecture people got adjusted into such jobs with their enormous experience in such fields. Like-wise in every category of occupation it is observed that the relevance of education to either job or income is of inverse nature to a larger extent. This is essentially true to the migrants to the West Asian countries in general and Kuwait is not an exception.

The category of professionals who were basically Engineers, Doctors, Architects and Computer analyst, even people with below graduation level were handling the professional jobs. It makes twenty per cent of such people who were just or below graduates. Many of them were from different faculties other than engineering, still became engineers in their cadres (see Table 3.16).

Table 3.15

Percent labour force by nationality and highest qualification in Kuwait

	Illiterate	*Read & Write*	*Primary School*	*Middle School*	*Secondary or equivalent*	*Graduate & above*	*Total*
Kuwaitis	36.4	14.3	21.7	16.2	9.0	2.4	100
Non-Kuwaitis	24.2	22.1	16.0	14.2	14.7	8.8	100
Hyderabadis	0.9	-	14.3	28.6	17.8	38.4	100
Total	28.9	19.0	18.1	15.1	12.5	6.4	100

Source: Annual Statistical Abstract, 1982 (Kuwait)

Sample Survey — 1990.

Table 3.16

Hyderabadi repatriate workers from Kuwait - By level of Education

	Illi trate	*< 4 class*	*4-8 class*	*8-10 class*	*> 10 class*	*Below Gra-duate*	*Gra-duate*	*Post Gra-duate*	*Medi-cine*	*Engi-neer-ing*	*Archi-tect-ive*	*Tech-nical diploma*	*Total*
Professional	-	-	-	-	-	9.1	18.2	-	13.6	36.4	9.1	12.6	100
Technical	3.3	6.7	16.7	16.7	23.3	3.3	20.0	10.0	-	-	-	-	100
Service & others	-	6.7	6.7	6.7	10.0	23.3	23.3	23.3	-	-	-	-	100
Drivers	-	40.0	30.0	30.0	-	-	-	-	-	-	-	-	100
Total	0.9	14.3	14.3	14.3	8.9	8.9	15.2	8.9	2.7	7.1	1.8	2.7	100

Source: Sample Survey — 1991.

The technical diploma-holders who are prone to take-up higher positions were only thirteen per cent of them and professional architects only nine per cent. The data shows not many doctors got attracted to Kuwait. However substantial number of engineering graduates were present in Kuwait.

The contingent of the technicians varied from illiterates to post-graduates. It is seen that seventy per cent of the technicians were matriculates passed. Since education does not hinder in the technical job as much as that of experience, hence to link education to technical job becomes invalid. That is why even post-graduates with experience have accepted technical service in Kuwait. This paid them well beyond their expectations hence, qualification and type of joy never went hand in hand.

Seventy per cent of the service personnel were below graduates to post-graduates. Naturally service activities involves more of education qualification. It is clear that there is the correlation existing between the service activities to that of level of education.

The category of drivers need more of experience than education. Good physical body and driving experience counts, as such hundred per cent of the drivers are below tenth class.

The overall educational background of the migrants show that forty five per cent of them were below matriculation standard. As many as thirty-three per cent are undergraduates. The remaining people with professional qualifications were handful and scattered.

A study on the "Inner city of Hyderabad" was made by Ratna Naidu (1986) the levels of education amongst the adults revealed predominantly in the muslim area shows 48.63% and 26.47% Illiterates in the slum and blighted areas of the city respectively. People who migrated to Kuwait (except 3.3% technicians) most of them were mostly literates. She has also shown that below tenth class 13.98% and 33.22% respectively in the slum and blighted areas. This amounts to 47.20%. The migrants to Kuwait in this category amounted to 51.8%. Similarly intermediate/diploma in technical training/graduates are 25.49% and the repatriates were 27.3%. Finally the post graduates of her study are 10.22% and the Kuwaiti migrants were 8.9%.

4
ECONOMIC CHARACTERISTICS OF HYDERABADI WORKERS REPATRIATED FROM KUWAIT

The labour migration across the national boundaries of India to various countries of the world is not a new phenomenon. The Indian relation with persian Gulf and South-East Asia, both in terms of trade and movement of people date backs to several centuries. The hallmark came with the abolition of slavery in India by the British. Independent labour from India moved into plantations and mining activities of Africa, SE Asia, Sri Lanka and Burma. This was a phenomenon of the 19th century migrations in India.

The twentieth century post independence period in India has witnessed the bifurcation of India and Pakistan, with mass exodus between the two countries. The composition of migrants in this phase was community, class-wise families and individuals. The independent India has witnessed a first phase of migration between 1950 to mid-1970. This comprised particularly the skilled, Technical and professionals emigration to Britain, United States, Canada and certain West European countries and Australia. The second phase of post independence labour movement has shown the semi-skilled workers at the beginning and the mid of 1970s. They started to migrate to the oil rich countries of South-West Asia. This phenomenon reached its peak by 1980s.

The Proctor General of Emigrants in the Ministry of Labour, provides emigration clearance to the workers intending to work abroad. This is the authentic source to obtain data on migration. However, emigration clearance is exempted for professionals, post-graduates and the persons who have already worked abroad for two years and the illegal migrants, who leave on visitor visa and succeed in staying back. Hence, accurate number of workers cannot be accounted for.

The data is available on the out-migration of labour from India. The annual out-flow has shown a minimum of 4000 in 1976 and reached a peak level of 275,000 in 1981, after which it has been declining. The 1986 annual labour outflow was 113649. Deepak (1989) has shown, the labour annual outflow from India to Kuwait in 1982 was 9764 and the outflow for 1984 and 1985 was 5466, 5512 respectively and in the year 1985, 4235 people left India to Kuwait. The estimated Indian workers in Kuwait was 32105 in the year 1975, it was 65,000 in 1979, in the year 1983 it was 115,000.

The geographical distribution of the indian workers in Kuwait in largely affected by the administrative and social aspects of the country. Besides, the locales of contract projects, the Indians are conspicuous in the Kuwait town. As the majority of the service oriented indian workers, house-maids and servants are found in the Kuwait town. The Kuwaiti 1975 census has shown that 16.1 per cent of the total population of Kuwait town were Indians. Kuwait city provides 50 per cent of the total jobs in the country, with 12.4 per cent of the total population, out of which 60.7 per cent are immigrants. (Al-moosa—1981). It is also noted that the distribution of Indian workers is in close resemblance to that of the Pakistanis and Iranians. Their concentration in Kuwait town, Salmiya and Howalli was respectively 39.3, 13.7 and 6.7 per cent of their total numbers in 1975.

The exodus of Indian workers to Kuwait was almost from all occupations. Since the need for semi-skilled and skilled personnel, along with that of the technicians and professionals was acute, almost every one with or without education or experience was provided with some or the other job. Kuwaitis were not willing to take up a number of works, hence, the immigrant labour of different countries filled the vacancy. Among the workers from India, it was the Keralites who formed 50 per cent of the emigrants from India to South-West Asian Countries. A large number of workers from almost every field of occupation moved into Kuwait.

The workers from Hyderabad have representative from secondary and tertiary sectors of economy. At the beginning it was the persons related to trade and commerce, illiterates, manual labour which has initiated the migratory movement. The petty traders and vendors of Hyderabad, who were available 16 hours a day on the road making business who could not satisfy the minimum requirements of their families. The illiteracy, big family size, lack or no investment potential in business, competitions in the business have created economic constraints to the most of the Muslim petty vendors. Initially the fruit sellers and other manual labourers, both in the market and the industries ventured to take a risk. They mortgaged their houses, gold, utensils and obtained loan on high interest rates to be paid to procure a passport and Visa.

The situation of the Indian labour by their prior occupation (before migration) in their home country/city and that in Kuwait is studied by Al-Moosa (1985) in his sample survey. The occupational percentage for the Hyderabadi workers is obtained through a sample survey conducted by the author at Hyderabad in 1991 (see Table 4.1).

The category of the professionals and technical workers emigrating India were capable to acquire almost the same profession as that of India. This was particularly true in case of the Doctors, Engineers, Computer specialists, Scientists and Architects. Since, there was no planned professional absorption, the immigrants in Kuwait had ample openings. The migrant from India was basically seeking employment with, the Kuwaiti Government as his first choice of selection. There were others, who wanted to obtain a "free Visa", this would enable them to select the best job as per the situation of wage and working.

The persons migrating on contract visa knew nothing about the host country. The only look-out is for the place of destination, type of job, wages, overtime of any and perks. They would only calculate the exchange of currency and what shall be their expenditure and how much could they save per month and send it to their families in India.

Given, such a situation the issue of Have's and Have nots in India was directly related. Those, who can lead a better social life with repute and economic self satisfaction and a sentimental attachments to their parents or spouses hesitated to migrate. Even such persons when were knowledged about the concessions, the pay package and

Table 4.1

Indian labour by occupation in their home country and in Kuwait

	Professional & Technical	*Administrative & Management*	*Clerical*	*Sales*	*Agriculture & Fisheries*	*Production & Labour*	*Services*	*Total*
1. In India	38.7	7.5	26.9	3.1	1.5	20.9	1.5	100
2. In Hyderabad	5.4	8.7	32.4	18.2	-	19.1	15.4	100
3. In Kuwait	33.3	4.8	29.8	8.3	-	14.3	9.5	100
4. Hyderabadi workers in Kuwait	4.8	5.8	23.5	30.6	-	28.3	7.0	100

Source: 1. Sample survey - All-moosa 1981

2. Sample survey - Hyderabad 1991.

facility to visit their home town annually made it a point to take a chance.

This mental or psychological readiness and willingness to migrate always plays a vital role in migration decision-making process. The professional were aware of their return status, they calculate the pros and cons of their migration and hence opt to move only on condition that they be well placed and excessively paid.

The situation of the Hyderabadi workers, particularly the professional remained the same as that of any other Indian citizen. The share of professional & technical personnel from Hyderabad remained (5.4%). The ambition of the Hyderabadi Doctors and Engineers is to go to U.K. or U.S.A. where they can earn more and find themselves suitable to their way of cultural society. In Gulf, the strict rules and regulations, the discipline, restriction of luxury and entertainment perhaps do not attract them to select South-West Asia as a first choice of migration. They always make efforts to land in some developed country of the world. However, the 4.8 per cent of the Hyderabadi professionals acquired the same professions as that of their home town.

The workers from administration and management 7.5 per cent from India and 8.7 per cent in Hyderabad, could not find the same job at Kuwait. They obviously shifted their occupation based on the availability of position, such people would illegally go for multiple jobs, hence, they go under the benefit of doubt.

The position of clerks from India was almost assured of their same position in Kuwait. The concept of Typist/Clerk/Accountant is that the three in one category of clerks who always found themselves attached to some office and table work. In case of the Hyderabadi clerks 32.4% only 23.5 per cent have acquired the same job. Others can be deemed to have shifted to sales and services, which generally has excess wage potential than a clerk.

The salesmen from India, 3.1 per cent had their sales experience in India. It can be presumed almost every one got the same job in Kuwait. The 8.3 per cent of Indians in Kuwait shows that, personnel from other fields have accepted salesmanship for extra income. The category of sales can be full time, part time, partnership, ownership and so on. Hence, workers willing to take part-time have better chances to obtain a salesman job. The sales persons from Hyderabad

18.2 per cent moved into Kuwait, but 30.6 per cent were found to be engaged in sales in Kuwait. This established the enterprising nature of the Hyderabadi workers.

The 1.5 per cent Indians with a background of agriculture and fishing work seen in some different occupations. Never, the Indian immigrants in Kuwait were seen in the primary sector of occupation.

Workers in the production and labour 20.9 per cent moved from India to Kuwait and 14.3 per cent stayed back in the same profession. The workers from Hyderabad 19.1 per cent went to Kuwait who worked as labour or in production activity were found in the same occupation. In fact 28.3 per cent of the Hyderabadi's, mostly drivers, welders, painters, turners, plumbers could obtain easy jobs in Kuwait.

The Service Oriented Personnel who left India were meagre (1.5%). However, in Kuwait 9.5 percent Indians in service shows that this category mainly comprised of women in addition to males from all categories. The migrants belonging to service category at Hyderabad (15.4%) did not take up the same job in Kuwait (7.0%). This is due to low wage and no extra or part time benefits. Hence, only people of middle age and women accepted service jobs.

Looney (1992) studied the "Manpower options in a small labour importing state: The influence of ethnic composition on Kuwaits development." His analysis was that in Kuwait the immigrants from Asia had grossly engaged in production and service sectors. The agriculture and allied activities were predominately engaged by the natives, the surrounding Nun-Kuwaiti Arabs who entered Kuwait in the first phase of migration.

Al-moosa (1981) found the indians in Kuwait have been engaged basically in three occupations in their country, 38.7 per cent in professional and technical work, 27 per cent clerks, 21 per cent production and transportation work. Besides Indians and Pakistanis are reluctant to join service due to language and social barriers. They are more concentrated in professional, technical labourers and transportation, this is due to either illiteracy or working language of English.

At Hyderabad, most of the Muslim community were working as bus, truck and auto drivers. They had a difficult time of more work and low wage. They were regarded as the best transport mechanics. Hence, predominantly those who left as drivers from Hyderabad found themselves suitable in the some job. Their percentage was quite substantial.

The situation in Kuwait on the occupational side is clear from the Annual Statistical Abstracts. In the year 1975, there were 71 per cent of the foreign labour component in all echelons of occupations. By 1982 the percentage raised to 79. The lower echelons of administration, clerks and manual labour also shows that in the year 1975 it was 85 per cent immigrant labour and the Abstract of 1982 has shown 92 per cent. Hence, the role of immigrants in the Kuwaits economy get more clearer, that the country's future and development is placed in the hands of the immigrant labour potential.

Immigrants women workers in Kuwait are very few in construction and transportation and allied sector (3%). But there is a quite sufficient number of women taking the service occupation. As already mentioned the service activity was mostly confined even from the Hyderabad into the service sector. The Hyderabadi women were found as Languages Translators, Tailors, Teachers, Computer Assistants and Nurses in Kuwait.

Multiple Occupations of the Immigrant Workers in Kuwait

The immigrant workers in Kuwait were subjected to by and large multiple occupations. Except those under contract bonds, professionals and those located too far from urban centres. The increase in income can be made possible only when employees take more, than one employment. Although there is legal ban on the migrants to go for more than one job.

Al-moosa (1981) observed on multiple employment in Kuwait by the immigrant workers as follows:

"Among the issue affecting total incomes of individuals that was not dealt with comprehensively by the survey was that of multiple occupations. There was natural reluctance on the part of respondents to give full answers to quarters concerning second and third occupations since this is frowned upon by employers and official entities. Only some ten percentage of the employees acknowledged earning from sources other than their principal occupation. It is believed that this is a serious under recording of the position. For Kuwait multiple employment of workers bring mixed benefits. On the other hand there must be suspicions that several employees get less than full dedication from their workers during normal working hours. Workers conserve their energy for the full spread of their occupations. This applies especially to the government sector. On the other hand it must be supposed that multiple employment enables Kuwait to do with less immigrant labour than it might do otherwise.

Yet there must be reservation on the whole matter of multiple employment. Because there is a legal ban on workers from abroad taking more than one job, there is little or no control on the second, third or other occupations. Quality of staff not scrutinized. Qualifications for these areas may well be significantly sub-standard. There is, in effect, an area of the so-called "black economy" an area of there is little return by way of taxation or other benefits to Kuwait. There is more than a slight suspicion that the government is given less than full measure from its foreign employees, largely as a result of multiple employment".

The multiple employment of Hyderabadi workers in Kuwait was responded by about 20 per cent. They confessed that the longer duration of stay, make them speak the Arabic workable language, besides the social and legal constraints also become known. Hence, the workers in the city are tend to accept petty jobs. Basically the respondents claimed that in the commercial activity, entertainment activity, there existed a large scope to avail part-time, obviously the increase in income collaborated with willing to accept more than one employment. This was true basically with workers having full time jobs as clerks, services and a few of the labourers and production workers.

Illegal Immigrant Workers in Kuwait

The illegal migrant workers found all over the South-West Asian countries. Their living in Kuwait as of other countries is subjected to extradiction if discovered. These workers stay in Kuwait very uncomfortably. There are paid very low wages, do not comprise in any of the Kuwaits welfare state system. They are very poorly housed. They are not documented by the survey teams, hence to approximate their number is not possible. However for working purpose it is assessed there were 40 to 50 thousand illegal workers in Kuwait by 1982. Results of the 1980 census suggest in broad terms that significant numbers of the work-force were unregistered, possibly between 10 to 15 per cent of the total of those actively employed. Three main categories were involved. 1. Illegal entrants smuggled into the state over land or sea border, 2. Persons who visited on visitor permits into the state and stayed back subsequently without permission, 3. Persons who entered on valid work permits but who stayed after these had expired. The problems posed by illegal workers have both economic and political dimensions for the Kuwaiti Government.

The number, causes, consequences and repercussions of Indian illegal workers in Kuwait calls for another detailed study. At Hyderabad, it is found that maximum number of workers have registered as Kuwaitis repatriates Association, their loses and produced their legal and authentic stay. Still, those who did not come forward to register, due to ignorance, or illegal stay or for other reasons cannot be confirmed as far as Hyderabadi illegal workers stayed in Kuwait.

Wage/Income Structure

The wage factor is a significant economic constraint of any migrant force. The financial reward is the ultimate factor of motivation and decision-making. The income structure of employees changes from Private to Government or Quasi Government. It also changes from type of job, risk involved, experience and so on. The existing pre-migration wages and income generating sources to a large extent provoke the migrants to take firm decision on the migration process.

The host country need to attract the workers of best quality as it is very difficult to destabilise skilled technicians from their home countries. It becomes quite necessary to attract the best skilled workers at all levels only through wage attraction. Hence, the type of labour received is directly related to the amount of wage paid.

The Indian work-force migrated to South-West Asia was heterogeneous in character. The semi-skilled, skilled, the technicians and the professionals were by and large able to procure better jobs and wages. In fact workers acquired a lots of skill related to indigenous requirement. This obviously created a situation to earn excess wages.

The Indian workers to Kuwait had the biggest factor of earning higher wages. The workers were aware of the truth that Kuwait was one of the richest country in the world and that it can provide wages more than their expectations. It cannot be ruled out that the Indian workers were lavishly paid in all the south-west Asian countries. It was only the factor of staying single or with family which was their major concern. The duration of stay, the educational background, the skill expertise age-sex structure are a few other variables which determined the wage structure of the migrants.

However, it is a universal truth that workers shall make a decision on migration only to earn as much as possible in a limited span of time and save as much as they can and return back to their home country where they can initiate a new process of rehabilitation. This is true in case of Migrant workers from India to south-west Asian in general and also of the Hyderabadis in particular.

The wages earned by individuals, families and communities differ radically by post to position. Each of these adopt a different approach of earning, living and saving. They are vigilant and are under surveillance of their employers. They never participate in the host country politics, or any other controversial issues. They mentally deem to be the honoured guests of the host country and they need to behave as non controversial individuals.

Earnings

The actual earnings of the immigrant workers in Kuwait is observed by Moosa (1981). A majority of them earned below KD 400 per month. The single house-hold members 67.3 per cent of them and the joint family house-hold members 45.6 per cent of them have earned below KD 400 per month. Those who earned below KD 100 are negligible in the joint families, but 4.1 per cent of the single members appeared in this brachet (see Table 4.2).

The individual family members were about 5.6 per cent but only 2.7 per cent of the joint family members earned above KD 800 per month. However, the 6.5 per cent also earned above KD 1000 or more per month. The less or more earnings as already mentioned is attributed to a large number of factors. Generally, both single and joint family members obviously attempt to earn as much as possible in a limited span of time. The joint family income is attached to the getting of families into Kuwait. Since the country stipulates an individual to earn above KD 400 per month to bring their spouse, hence the male members in the joint family as an individual is deemed to

Table 4.2

Distributions of monthly income from main and other occupations of heads of house-holds and joint-family units (KD%) of the immigrant workers in Kuwait

	Less than 100	*100 199*	*200 299*	*300 399*	*400 499*	*500 599*	*600 699*	*700 799*	*800 899*	*900 999*	*1000 or more*
Single house-hold %	4.1	16.4	25.3	21.5	13.4	7.3	3.3	3.1	5.6	-	-
Joint family house-hold %	0.2	5.6	17.7	22.1	17.9	13.9	7.4	3.7	2.7	2.3	6.5

Source : Sample survey - Al-moosa 1981.

KD = Kuwaiti Dinar.

be earning the targeted income as per the Kuwait law to get their families.

The Kuwaiti law is subjected to change with the earning capacity of the Kuwaiti Dinar (KD). This also means extra efforts on the part of the individuals to strive for more earnings constantly to retain his family for a longer duration of stay.

The highly educated professionals and those who had already a longer duration of stay and who had reached a substantial earning capacity are considered dare to get in their families to Kuwait. Certain welfare measures provided by the government and the private company perks are enjoyed by the family members during their stay as Kuwait. The embassy schools, the health facility and free accommodation are the major concessions, which in fact are dearer in Kuwait. Individuals speculate the future prospects of their position before they plan to stay with families in Kuwait.

On the other hand, there are a large number of married household members, although earning above KD 400 per month, prefer to leave their families behind. These people acknowledge that the family members and the children get disturbed due to change, adaptation to new environment, additional concentration on children, the social ethos of the country and the economic constraint of high expenditure are a few issues which discourage them to stay with families in Kuwait. Instead they prefer annual or bi-annual visits of 45 or 60 days.

The bachelors aim to stay unmarried for a longer period. They calculate the difficulties which arise due to marriage. They constantly attempt to save more money and, procure worthy assets, for a comfortable stay, purchase a plot, house and other house-hold assets. Besides the bachelors are over burdened with the joint responsibilities of the family, like sisters marriages, education for the younger brothers, help financially the weaker lots of the kith and kin, Holy pilgrimage to Mecca and Madina of the age-old parents. Most of such responsibilities keep the bachelors pre-occupied and hence their earnings and the family expectations from them goes proportional. This is the observed conditions of the Hyderabadi bachelor workers in Kuwait.

Distribution of Income of the Head of the House-hold of the Hyderabadi Worker Before and After Migration to Kuwait

Single Family House-hold (Income)

A large chunk of the Head of the House-hold members before migration of about 78 per cent earned about Rs. 1000 per month. The survey shows about 0.1 per cent were earning around Rs. 5000 per month. This overall total situation suggests that workers in Hyderabad could earn as much as Rs. 5000 per month as maximum, whereas in Kuwait this much amount is the minimum earning.

The distribution of income before migration of all the occupational workers was almost coming with that of the average, except service workers above 80 per cent of them earned above average. This was due to their service in the government. Most of them working as Clerks/Typists were in this bracket.

Earnings at Hyderabad were associated with a number of factors. The educational status to some extent was a factor, but technical or general skill is a pre-requisite to better earning. Unlike the service people, those who had skill were working 12 hours a day and often over time to earn more.

The Hyderabadi migrant workers to Kuwait initiated with those who had certain expertise of skill and technical know-how in the construction work. Hence, welders, masons, turners and allied workers had no dearth of jobs. The category of drivers also attracted a very large number of the government employed drivers to either obtain lien or leave or even abstain from duties to migrate for more earning.

The second stream, a rather parallel flow of a few service workers along with those of technicians had a certain scope and low wages than professionals. These workers due to their easy jobs but low wages had sufficient extra time and energy which they started to utilise for second or third employment. The commercial establishment allowed the part-time jobs and also a few construction projects. Hence, the illegal or multiple employment was often available in the evenings (see Table 4.3).

The post migration earnings of the migrants to Kuwait of the Hyderabadi workers is shown in Table 4.4. Most of the workers income of all occupational categories ranged between Rs. 5000-50,000 per month. There were very few who earned less than Rs. 5000 or more than Rs. 50,000 per month except the professionals, all the minimum of the professionals earnings was about Rs. 20000 per month. 54.5 per cent of the professionals had their earnings between 30 to 50 thousand rupees per month, only about 4.5 per cent earned below Rs. 20,000 per month.

Table 4.3

Per cent income distribution of the head of the house-hold of the Hyderabadi worker before migration to Kuwait

Category	*< 500*	*501-1000*	*1001-2000*	*2001-5000*	*> 5000*	*Total*
Professionals	27.4	50.0	13.6	4.5	4.5	100
Technicians	26.7	43.3	16.7	13.3	-	100
Servicians	23.3	63.3	10.0	3.4	-	100
Drivers	23.3	53.3	23.4	-	-	100
Total	25.3	52.8	16.4	5.4	0.1	100

Source: Sample Survey Hyderabad — 1991.

Above 90 per cent of the technicians, service people, drivers earned below Rs 30,000 per month during their stay at Kuwait. There exists a benefit of doubt of these category of workers that they earned all this income through a single source. They might have had several other services as well to earn this much of income (see Table 4.4).

Table 4.4

Per cent income distribution of the head of the house-hold of the Hyderabadi worker after migration to Kuwait

Category	*< 5000*	*5001-10000*	*10001-20000*	*20001-30000*	*30000-50000*	*> 50000*	*Total*
Professionals	-	-	4.5	18.2	54.5	22.7	100
Technicians	3.3	30.0	40.0	20.0	6.7	-	100
Servicians	6.7	13.3	40.0	30.0	10.0	-	100
Drivers	-	36.7	43.3	20.0	-	-	100
Total	3.0	21.3	34.0	22.0	15.2	4.5	100

Source: Sample Survey Hyderabad — 1991.

Joint Family House-holds (Income) Occupation-wise

The concept of joint family house-holds is common amongst the Asians unlike the western culture, Asians for various reasons are compelled to live in joint family system. The cooperation between the members of the latter system is both social and economic. Generally under the steward ship of the Head of the family most of the decisions of the house-hold matters is taken and the other members usually co-operate.

The joint family house-hold income gets blurred due to the number of earners, dependents and expenditure pattern. Hence, the ideal would have been to obtain statistics of the number of earners, dependents, total income. However, under this study, the total income of all of the joint family, without ascertaining the earners or dependents is considered (see Table 4.5).

Table 4.5

Per cent income distribution of the head of the joint house-hold of the Hyderabadi worker before immigration to Kuwait

Category	*< 500*	*501-1000*	*1001-2000*	*2001-5000*	*> 5000*	*Total*
Professionals	4.5	4.5	22.7	50.0	18.3	100
Technicians	10.0	36.7	26.7	6.6	20.0	100
Servicians	36.7	30.0	16.7	10.0	6.6	100
Drivers	16.7	50.0	33.3	-	-	100
Total	18.0	32.0	24.0	15.3	10.7	100

Source : Sample Survey Hyderabad — 1991.

The 75 per cent of the joint families before migration irrespective of the earners had a monthly income of Rs. 2000 per month. 10.7 per cent of the house-holds earned above Rs. 5000 per month of income. Regarding the professional joint family households, 50 per cent fell under the bracket of Rs. 2000-5000 per month and 18.3 per cent had over Rs. 5000 per month of income. This occupational category was deemed to be earners of satisfactory wages. Also such house-holds had more earners including women and less dependents, also had more assets of their own. The members of these house-holds migrate only on assurance of high salary perks and free annual visits to the home country. Often, the migration of the established professionals like Doctors and Engineer is difficult unless the attraction at the other side is more. A small per cent of the professionals holding joint families were earnings altogether less than Rs. 1000 per month.

It is also observed that the Technicians, Service and Drivers joint families were predominantly under the income range of Rs. 2000 per month. However, 20 per cent of the technician joint family households had income of Rs. 5000 per month and above. These categories had less earners and more dependents.

The service oriented personnel 36.7 per cent had less than Rs. 500 per month of joint family income before migration. Hence, it is observed that such people initiated to learn certain technical skill which is in demand in the middle east and attempt to migrate. The joint family house-holds after migrating to Kuwait have shown, 75 per cent of all such families earned upto Rs. 30,000 per month. A meagre 3.6 per cent earned less than Rs. 5000 per month.

The professional joint family house-holds 54.5 per cent were conspicuous in the bracket of Rs. 30,000-50,000 per month. None of such house-holds had less than Rs. 20,000 income per month. However, 18.2 per cent of them have shown their income figures beyond Rs. 50,000 per month.

The Technicians 70 per cent of them earned upto about Rs. 20,000 per month and only 6.4 per cent had their incomes above Rs. 50,000 per month. The service personnel are found under all the income brackets 10 per cent of them earned is less than Rs. 50,000 per month, however a majority of 33.3 per cent were in the bracket of Rs. 20,000-30,000 per month.

The category of drivers and technicians of 43.3 per cent each are in the bracket of Rs. 20,000-30,000 per month. However 36.7 per cent of the Drivers joint families had income between Rs. 5000-10,000 per month of income. Never the drivers earned above Rs. 30,000 per month of income (see Table 4.6).

Al-moosa (1985) in his survey, established the fact that the immigrant labour income in Kuwait is directly proportional to their education. He also showed the relationship between duration of stay and age varies in income. His survey on income verses education had shown, the illiterates and those who can read and write 31.1 per cent and 10.0 per cent respectively earned less than KD 100 per month. In contrast to this only 0.4 per cent of the immigrant workers were found in this bracket. Similarly on the upper bracket, those who earned above KD 800 per month were 1.4 per cent of those who can read and write and 10.7 per cent of the post graduates. Hence, it is established that the income and education are directly proportional.

Table 4.6

Per cent Income distribution of the head of the joint household of the Hyderabadi worker after migration to Kuwait

Category	*< 5000*	*5001-10000*	*10001-20000*	*20001-30000*	*30000-50000*	*> 50000*	*Total*
Professionals	-	-	-	27.3	54.5	18.2	100
Technicians	-	26.7	43.3	6.8	16.8	6.4	100
Servicians	10.0	16.7	23.3	33.3	13.3	3.4	100
Drivers	3.3	36.7	43.3	16.7	-	-	100
Total	3.6	21.4	29.5	20.5	19.0	6.0	100

Source : Sample Survey Hyderabad — 1991.

Regarding the duration of stay and the income pattern, it is evident that those who stayed below 5 years, 75 per cent of them were earning between KD 100-300 per month. While those who stayed between 5 to 9 years, 80 per cent of them had their income between KD 100-400 per month. This situation remained constant for those who stayed since 15 years, and above. Hence, it shows that, a stay of about 10 years in average can achieve maximum possible income and thereafter it remains constant irrespective of the increase in the length of stay.

The age versus income of the immigrant workers has shown that those who were below 20 years predominantly earned below KD 200 per month. Those between 20-30 years, 85 per cent of them earned between KD 100-400 per month. This followed by those aged between 30 to 40 years, 90 per cent of them earned between KD 100-600 per month. This was the effective age group with maximum earning capacity. However, the higher aged workers above 40 years above 7 per cent of them were earning above KD 800 per month. Meagre 2 per cent of these had their income below KD 100 per month.

Age and income relations appears to be the result of experience and energy potential. Workers between 30-40 years possess more energy and they with their Arabic language expertise and the required experience to go for a single, double or multiple employment. Obviously, the earnings go higher and higher due to this.

Moosa in his survey observed that the income of the Asian group of workers as follows:

"In the Asian group, the migrants are deeply involved in the lower paid grades of manual labour and/or clerical jobs, with 56 per cent earning less than KD 300 per month and 92 per cent earning less than KD 400 per month. There were also small numbers who were in the most well-paid bracket. Among the worst-paid groups in Kuwait were the Asians from countries other than India and Pakistan. Some 35 per cent earned less than KD 100 per month and more than half were paid less than KD 300 per month. Other nationalities served to be employed mainly in well paid work. More than half of them earned more than KD 600 per month."

Comparative Wages Paid by the Government for Kuwaiti and Non-Kuwaiti Workers

The Kuwaiti annual statistical Abstract, 1981 has shown the Average salaries paid by the government for various occupational categories, for the year 1976. A clear cut distinction is find between the Kuwaiti workers wages and the non-Kuwaiti workers are paid less. A major observation is that a Kuwaiti semi-skilled or unskilled labour, production labour, labour in agriculture and clerical are well paid by the government, which is closely equivalent to that of a non-Kuwaiti professional worker. As already noted that the workers employed as labourers in their home countries were found in high occupations like professionals and technicians in Kuwait. This is due to their early migration to Kuwait and learning the professional skill at the earliest and grabing a job (see Table 4.7).

The differences of wages between the Kuwaiti and non-Kuwaiti individual male member depicts that his wages are subjected to his education, age, duration of stay, type of employment. Hence, the table does not take into consideration all such factors given above. It is only point of analysis on wage differences.

Table 4.7

Average salaries paid by the Government 1976 (KD/month)

Sl. No.	*Occupational Category*	*Kuwaiti Average*	*Non-Kuwaitis Average*
1.	Technical Professions	239	206
2.	Other Professions	251	190
3.	Managers	556	503
4.	Executive and Clerical	198	158
5.	Sales etc.	162	80
6.	Agriculture and Fisheries	191	69
7.	Production Workers	220	106
8.	Labourers Semi-shifted	202	63
9.	Unskilled Labourer	189	67
	Total - All Groups	204	123

Source : Annual Statistical Abstract - Kuwait - 1987.

The high wages paid to the Kuwaiti worker by the government in all sectors of employment is a policy matter. The Kuwaiti Government pays special allowances to its indigenous labour, obviously, the repercussions on the indigenous labour improvement appear bleak. The lower labour group of workers and those in technical and professional group, there exist hardly any substantial wage difference. The minimum was KD 189 per month for the Kuwaiti unskilled labour and a technical professional worker is paid KD 239 per month at average. This meagre wage difference for both creates a lots of disappointment and discourage indigenous labour improvement. The only lavishly paid category was that of the managers, irrespective of a Kuwaiti or non-Kuwaiti does not show much wage difference.

The non-Kuwaiti workers average wages were found to be below KD 100 per month for categories of sales etc. Agriculture and fisheries, semi-skilled and unskilled labourers. Hence, the majority of immigrant work force would naturally prefer to go for private contract work than for the Government sector. The non-Kuwaitis had better wages paid only for Managers, Technical and other professions.

Differentials of this kind have led in the past to Kuwait being described as wage slavery economy.

The lower wage acceptance by the non-Kuwaiti workers is associated with fears of deportation. In the year 1980 some 9651 persons and in the year 1982 about 50,000 persons were deported under an amnesty for foreigners contravening residence regulations (Moosa 1981).

The non-Kuwaiti workers in addition to fear of deportation are also under the fear of resignation repercussions, since there is no organization to protect them. Foreign workers are not permitted to group together in trade unions.

The uneasy job situation, wage dissatisfaction, the fear of return migration and rehabilitation and unforeseen constraints and consequences always keep firm mental grip on the foreign workers. Only the long duration of stay, adequate savings in the home country and with no other liabilities can the foreigners feel contended. For others, it is an unknowns bondage and he has to be conscious of consequences and repercussions.

To assess, the fear complexity and the level of satisfaction, living in Kuwait of the foreign workers was elicited by Moosa (1981). He found in all 68.9 per cent of them were satisfied, 27.2 per cent more or less satisfied and 3.9 per cent dissatisfied with life in Kuwait.

The males 71.8 per cent were satisfied 24.1 per cent more or less satisfied and 4.1 per cent were dissatisfied. The female 68.3 per cent were satisfied, 27.8 per cent more or less satisfied and 3.9 dissatisfied.

Expenditure Pattern of the Hyderabadi Workers in Kuwait

The expenditure pattern of any house-hold is reflected in terms of total income, number of dependents. Consumption pattern, the expenditure pattern is prone to change occupation-wise. The rural and urban house-holds differ in consumption pattern. Hence, to relate expenditure, (which is a dependent variable) with that of income (independent variable) estimates a certain pattern emerges. The consumption pattern of all the house-holds has shown a remarkable change in terms of expenditure. The post migration trend is associated with more expenditure accompanied with luxuries, than the essential commodities, the consumption pattern was reverse prior to migration.

It is also found that the expenditure is also related to the size of the house-hold, literacy, age and sex structure, assets already in possession, own house and so on.

Monthly income of the house-hold was not only from the main and subsidiary occupations. It was also derived from house-rents, pensions, remittances from abroad and so on. The needs and wants changed from community/group/individual as well. For example the muslim community had a different expenditure and consumption pattern than others. The house-holds of the muslims were mostly joint families with large dependency ratio, large number of inmates per room, small houses, high consumption levels, low income, high indebtedness are the common characteristics. The other communities obviously had a different pattern of living standards and consumption pattern altogether.

The muslim community go for a lots of criminal wastage of money, food clothing and so on. Celebrate large number of feasts and functions, marriage functions are too expensive, majority of this community has inherited the consumption and expenditure behaviour from their ancestors and their society. Even the births and death ceremonies are costly affairs. Hence, in a given situation where the house-hold incomes are low and high expenditure leads to indebtedness or selling away of old antiques, utensils, mortgage of gold ornaments, house and so on is a common scenario of the muslim community in general and that of the Hyderabadi muslim in particular.

In continuation of the above discussion, it is observed that the muslim youth is very emotional, sensitive, fundamentalist, robed with illiteracy or low literacy, possess a certain skill generally inherited from their forefathers or own a small shop, unceremoniously start off earning at any age. A large number of muslim child labour is conspicuous in the informal sector all over the city. They are visible as motor mechanics, flower weavers, cycle repairers, wprlomg on a certain cottage industries, assistants in the commercial and hotel business.

Given a brief background of the muslim community, it becomes quite a necessity to go for more and more earning for the male members. The youth, the middle aged all of them are willing to migrate usually, long distance and save maximum to meet the growing expenditure of their house-hold. Obviously, when the Gulf opportunities aroused, the workers from all fields explored at a maximum and that are Hyderabadis found almost in every country of the South-West Asia. The muslim community generally discourage female work participation.

Pattern of Expenditure in Kuwait

An attempt is made to elicit from the Hyderabadi workers in Kuwait, staying single and those who lived along with their families. This brought out a situation in contrast to their home-town living. Excess of expenditure is recorded in terms of accommodation. The bachelors, who are under contract, however had no problem of boarding, lodging and free health facility. But for those who are not in possession of such facility were spending excessively.

Single Member House-hold

In Kuwait always a couple of workers got closer and decided to stay in a house. The expenditure on rent, electricity bill was shared among all of them. Even in case of the purchase of groceries for daily consumption was co-operative. Hence it was noted from the respondents the pattern of expenditure and savings based on their monthly incomes (see Table 4.8).

Table 4.8

Per cent monthly expenditure pattern of the single member house-hold Hyderabadi worker residing at Kuwait (Income-wise)

Monthly income in Rupees	*Accomodation electricity etc.*	*Groceries and kirana*	*Transport*	*Education of the children*	*Personal*	*Savings/ Remittances*
< = 10,000	25%	10%	5%	-	10%	50%
10,001-20,000	28%	14%	8%	-	10%	40%
20,001-30,000	24%	15%	5%	18%	10%	28%
30,001-50,000	35%	12%	8%	15%	13%	17%
> 50,000	18%	5%	2%	12%	5%	58%

It is evident from the Table 4.8 that members earning below Rs. 10,000 per month spent 50 per cent on accommodation, transport, groceries and personal and the rest was saved or remitted to the home country. Those members who earned between Rs. 10,000 to 20,000 per month had more expenditure on accommodation and groceries and 40 per cent remained under saving of their total monthly income.

Family Expenditure

The pattern of family expenditure in Kuwait remained entirely different than their home-town, obviously, the dependency of members mostly wife and children and their educational and health care coupled with rent on accommodation become dearer, since school education in Kuwait is free there was expenditure on tution. The monthly expenditure on groceries was also high.

As already mentioned, that immigrants in Kuwait are entitled to bring their family if their monthly income is above KD 400 per month. This figure is subjected to change with the change in Kuwaiti Dinar value. Hence members who lived along with their families in Kuwait spent according to their income brackets. It is also observed that the accommodation expenditure was directly related to the number of family members, earners and dependents. Hence, high expenditure in Kuwait is reflected to low savings and low remittances. A majority of the migrants preferred to retain their families in the hometowns.

The saving pattern registered amongst the house-holds staying in Kuwait with families have shown 28%, 17% and 58% respectively for the families whose income ranged between Rs. 20 to 30 thousand, 30 to 50 thousand and above Rs. 50,000 per month respectively.

Luxurious Assets of the Hyderabadi Workers Before and After Migration to Kuwait

The better standard of living is associated with in possession of certain luxurious assets, the purchase of items such as car, colour TV, VCP/VCR, cooking range, air coolers, air conditioner, deck system, telephone, scooter etc. become indicators of luxurious living. In order to procure these items, obviously the earnings and savings of the workers result into the possession of these assets. At an outset it is clear that a majority of the house-holds of Hyderabadi workers before migration were never in possession of even the essential items and assets. It was only after migration, that they could afford to purchase (see Table 4.9).

It is evident from Table 4.9 the telephone was available with certain professionals and a few of the technicians before migration, but later after migration their number has increased. Basically, the professionals if employed with Government service shall be provided with a telephone facility. Other maintain a telephone for their social contacts and emergency calls and so on. However, the people in service jobs and the drivers were having a telephone even after migration.

The facility of a car, except 13.6 per cent of the professionals none had before migration. However, there is a car in possession of a majority of the workers who migrated and on arrival back purchased a car. The drivers category was more particular to own a car, since, they speculated its income generating capacity in their absence and that it shall be an asset in case of their permanent return migration.

Possession of electronic goods like colour TV, VCR/VCP is conspicuous with a large number of the workers after migration. However, the drivers house-hold did not pay much attention to such items, since they either cannot afford or that they are really not willing to own. Their illiterate family members cannot maintain or operate, hence they are not interested in such costly and delicate instruments. The tendency with regards to other luxuries assets has also shown, that a larger chunk of the workers were in a capacity to own. But they preferred to invest money in purchase of gold, plots, house renovation. Hence, it can be concluded that the post migration positively showed a tremendous change in their life style. The after migration changed not only in their physical outlook, but also psychological awareness and importance of better and decent living. Their children's education, purchase of necessary assets out of their savings is recorded during the survey process.

Skill Potential and Change of Occupation of the Immigrant Workers in Kuwait with Special Reference to Hyderabadi Workers

Apart from the professional and scientific personnel on the one side and unskilled labour in all fields, the possession of a certain technical skill which has an employment utility role in Kuwait, was sought after much by the migrants. Majority of the Hyderabadi workers learnt the required skill within a limited time, acquired certificate of

Table 4.9

Per cent House-hold luxurious assets of Hyderabadi workers before and after migration (Occupation-wise)

	Tele-phone	*Car*	*Scooter*	*Color T.V.*	*VCP/ VCR*	*Cooking Range*	*Air Cooler*	*Air condi-tioning*	*Deck System*	*Gold & Jewellery*	
Professionals	BM	22.7	13.6	81.8	27.3	13.6	22.7	45.5	9.0	9.0	36.4
	AM	54.5	45.5	100	100	68.2	100	100	54.5	27.3	100
Technicians	BM	6.7	-	33.3	-	-	-	16.7	-	-	16.7
	AM	33.3	26.7	100	100	100	100	66.7	16.7	33.3	100
Servicians	BM	-	-	16.7	3.3	-	-	6.7	-	-	6.7
	AM	10	10	100	83.3	50	33.3	33.3	10	-	100
Drivers	BM	-	-	6.7	-	-	-	3.3	-	-	-
	AM	-	33.3	50	16.7	-	-	3.3	-	-	26.7
Total	BM	6.3	2.7	31.3	6.3	16.1	4.5	16.1	1.8	1.8	13.4
	AM	22.3	27.7	86.6	73.2	53.6	55.4	47.3	19.6	16.1	86.6

experience with private firms. This provided ample opportunity to procure a contract visa for migration. The construction projects in hand in Kuwait called upon a specialized workers who can fill in the gap of a skilled technician. The migrants obviously keeping the type of skill in demand started to learn the some extensively. The language of arabic and English were also considered as skills to consolidate in a better job in Kuwait.

The decision to migrate also had its impact in the existing employment of occupation. Most of the school students started to attend skill schools privately organized with a desire to migrate. Other who were employed either private or government also initiated to learn Arabic and English language, computers, driving and other skills in demand. Hence, the city of Hyderabad is seen to have a number of such skill centres.

In Kuwait, there appeared a distinction between the Asians, Arabs and allied personnel concentrated in certain activities, whilst, the Europeans and Americans preferred to opt certain exclusive jobs which retained their cultural image despite a stay in a foreign country. The most affected by culture were the Asians, who willingly accepted the emerging new culture in the foreign country.

Moosa (1981) in his survey attempted to find the relationship between main occupations in country of origin and in Kuwait. He observed that there was a close correlation between the occupations at the country of origin and in Kuwait in his sample survey. However, when he looked from the criterion of the proportion of the group actually following their original occupations in Kuwait, he did find that the correlation was weak (see Table 4.10).

Moosa analysed that only 68 percent of the total workers remained with their original occupations in Kuwait. He found 89 percent of the professional and technical personnel retained their occupations on arrival into Kuwait. The other workers predominantly showed a change in their home country employment and that in Kuwait.

Surprisingly, Moosa was able to trace out that a majority of the workers who were basically labourers in their home country found themselves in high positions in Kuwait. It was already seen even in terms of income, the illiterates and those who can read and write were able to earn beyond KD 400 per month. In contrast to this, the genuine skilled and experienced workers in their home countries were placed

Table 4.10

Relationship between main occupations in the country of origin and in Kuwait

Occupation in the country of origin	*Occupation in Kuwait*														
	Profess-ional & Techni-cal		*Administra-tive and Manage-ment*		*Clerical and Execu-tive*		*Sales*		*Services*		*Agricul-ture & Fishe-ries*		*Production and Labour*		*Total*
	No.	*%*	*No.*	*%*	*No.*	*%*	*No.*	*%*	*No.*	*%*	*No.*	*%*	*No.*	*%*	*No.*
1. Professional and Technical	411	88.7	10	2.2	29	6.3	8	1.7	1	0.2	-	-	4	0.9	463
2. Administrative and Managerial	20	45.5	16	36.3	7	15.9	1	2.3	-	-	-	-	-	-	44
3. Clerical and Executive	26	20.6	10	7.9	70	55.6	4	3.2	6	4.8	-	-	10	7.8	126
4. Sales	12	15.6	6	7.8	8	10.4	35	45.4	5	6.5	1	1.3	10	13.0	77
5. Services	1	2.2	2	4.4	5	11.1	2	4.4	21	46.8	-	-	14	31.1	45
6. Agriculture & Fishing	3	2.8	2	2.0	13	12.7	9	8.8	23	22.6	8	7.8	44	43.2	102
7. Production & Labour	12	6.5	5	2.7	3	1.6	14	7.5	7	3.8	-	-	145	77.9	186
8. Total	485	46.5	51	4.9	135	12.9	73	7.0	63	6.0	9	0.9	227	21.8	1043

Source : Sample Survey (1981) A1-moosa.

at subordinate levels. The professionals and technical personnel also were prepared to accept any work lesser to their capacity.

Further, the survey also showed the differences between males and females in occupational status in their country of origin and in Kuwait. 90 per cent of the women migrated from different countries of origin had their background of professional, technical and clerical skill. However, a large number of them were found to be engaged in other activities related to labour.

The agriculture and fisheries sector was one such case, where almost 89 per cent of them were in their original field of employment. Similar trend was also associated with that of the production and labour category of workers. A high degree of flexibility affected all other groups, with more than half of all those from any other employment category in their home countries were replaced with other categories of occupations in Kuwait.

The occupational change (mobility) of the Hyderabadi workers in Kuwait is already discussed. The trend has shown the professional technical, administrataive and managerial occupations retained their same job in Kuwait. None from agriculture background entered into the primary economy of Kuwait, large number, who had service occupations in their home country joined the production and labour sector and also that of sales sector.

The foreign labour in Kuwait in terms of skills appears to be self reinforcing. Kuwait need to always plan for the guest workers in terms of physical, politico and socio-economic conditions of the immigrants. The syndrome of dependency by the Kuwaitis on the foreign labour is both their weakness and their strength. The economic diversification of the state, the adaptation of developmental plans, all such programmes are associated with the foreign skill in hand. However, the final option of immigrant policies, residential laws, wage laws and other concessions and restrictions are in the hands of the Kuwaits policy numbers. This they shall do with the changing needs and circumstances arising from time to time.

5
HOUSING CHARACTERISTICS OF HYDERABADI REPATRIATED WORKERS FROM KUWAIT

The chapter aim at the study of housing characteristics of Hyderabadi Kuwaitis while they were in Kuwait and when have returned to their home city. The first section is based on the information collected from secondary sources and from the conformation provided by the Kuwaitis who had returned.

Housing Conditions of Immigrant Workers in Kuwait

Food, clothing and shelter are deemed as the essential prerequisites for average living. The migrant workers at the country of destination, particularly in the towns and cities, accessible to their work place, face a tremendous housing problem. The single member problem is different than those staying with families. The government policy on housing, the rental laws, availability of space and other planning issues always impose new constraints and restraints.

In Kuwait, the government concern on housing problem is two fold. On the one hand, they keep the local Kuwaiti housing needs, type, location, ethnic segregation and on the other side, the non-Kuwaiti housing problem, particularly, building of bachelor and multistorey apartments with suitable resident-work place locations. The building types of the Kuwaiti and non-Kuwaitis need to be remained separate.

The government of Kuwait has imposed the house lease law allowing owners to increase property rents by upto 100 per cent for every five years. The law also states that the owner has the right to demolish the building after 25 years. Obviously this aggravates the problem, for the owner constantly exercises his rights and demolish old house to construct multi-storey buildings. This may on the one side create more of construction employment demand at the cost of acute housing shortage until the new structures emerge.

Housing problem is regarded as one of the reasons for restriction of inflow of new migrants into Kuwait. The contractors, who bring the labour from abroad also are put under trouble with the housing policies and conditions charging.

The housing law further states that only Kuwaiti nationals are permitted to own the title of real estate, whether land or housing. Even long-term residents with 20 to 25 years spent continuously in Kuwait have no right to become House owners. There is a strong feeling among many of the expatriate community, that legal possession of ownership for those with long standing residence does not be inimical to Kuwaits prosperity.

The problem of separate housing for locals and immigrants has certain, social, political, technical and financial constraints. The increasing immigrant labour from various countries also demand separate tenants for Asians, Europeans, Americans, the individual vast space villas, the multi-storey apartments are two different sides of the housing types. The immigrant workers at the beginning started to concentrate around the Kuwait city peripheries, later they are further pushed back.

The government decision to renovate and develop the old Kuwait city as a centre for official, political, administrative and economic centre, huge compensation and land outskirts the city was provided to the owners. In turn the owners were left to design their gift lands for appropriate use. In Kuwait the government did not enter the housing market but let it to the private sector, hence, housing has become a lucrative profitable investment sector.

The acute shortage and high housing rent imposed heavy restrictions in the immigrant workers who planned to bring their families. Those who already are staying with families started to send them back to their home country. Heavy expenditure was incurred on housing, education and medicine, this became a family push factor for a larger number of medium waged workers who were not guaranteed any housing facility through either the employer or the contractor.

Free housing as provided by the employer is of two types. The university professors and consultants are given free quarters without any deductions from pay. The other category of free housing is for teachers and doctors, but a part of their portion of income is deducted towards housing rent.

The wages of the workers increase by certain percentage from time to time, but there is a disproportionate increase in the housing rents. 30 per cent wage increase leads to 100 per cent increase for old property and 300 per cent increase for new property. In average 20 per cent of the income of the migrant is paid towards housing, 89.3per cent of the immigrant families in Kuwait paid rent directly from their wage earnings (Moosa 1981). The housing rent for 7.7 per cent of Indian workers in Kuwait was paid by the employer and 92.3 per cent paid the housing rent by themselves.

The geographical separation between the host and the Guest communities remains a vital factor in the housing needs of Kuwait. The latter who were previously concentrated in old Kuwait city, where their housing quality and quantity was discouraging. The Kuwaiti community with its traditional, tribal and a different socio-economic structure, ethnic identity, language and cultural safety preferred not to mix with the vast immigrant nationalities, hence, the laws of housing ownership in favour of the natives is prepared.

Although, both the locals and immigrants share their views on work-place and for administrative reasons, but socio-economic and geographical segregation, restrict housing types, is leading to excessive social and geographical separation between the two communities with increase of time.

The immigrant population in Kuwait are found nearly in all residential settlements, there are areas designated as non-Kuwaiti as well. However, segregation based on nationalities is not so conspicuous, but it is characterised by certain type of houses, rent paying capacity, free housing, stay with family or bachelor decides the location and type of residential quarter of stay.

Monthly Housing Rent Paid by the emigrate Workers in Kuwait

The average monthly rental payment by the various nationals of immigrant workers in Kuwait is given by Moosa (1981). The Indian workers in Kuwait were the second largest housing rent community followed by the others (Europeans, Americans, etc.). The average rent paid by the latter was KD 150 per month and the Indians in average paid KD 128.5 per month. The Pakistanis average rental payment was only KD 85.3 per month. The higher side of rental payment by the Indians endorses that they can afford for a better house and are capable of bringing their family with them. This appears to be absent of the Pakistanis (see Table 5.1).

It is also observed that none of the Indians pay below KD 30 per month towards house rent, 15.8 per cent of the Pakistanis are found in this category. 27 per cent of the Indians pay between KD 30-70 house rent per month, whilst 52.6 per cent of the Pakistanis fall under this range.

In the higher payment of the rentals, we find the Indians 52 per cent of them pay between KD 110-150 and the Pakistanis in the same range represent 26.3 per cent. Another 2.1 Indians are capable of paying as much as KD 230 per month, wherein none of the Pakistanis appear paying this much of housing rent. Hence, it can be concluded that the Indians were living in better houses than the Pakistanis. In fact, the Indian housing conditions are closer to that of any other western developed country national housings.

Housing Density of the Immigrant Workers in Kuwait

Increase of the immigrant workers is reflected in living standards, payment of house rents and housing density, Moosa (1981) found the following pattern of the Housing densities of the immigrant workers in Kuwait. It is found that in Kuwait the highest housing density is among the Palestinians, with 2.6 persons per room and the lowest among the Europeans 0.93 persons per room. Indians, Egyptians and Pakistanis lie between these two extremes (see Table 5.2).

The rental payment is directly related to the Housing density. The Europeans and Americans (others) 70.4 per cent of each person live in one or less than one room. The situation for Indians is about 80 per cent of each of the individuals have more or less than one room, its a close figure to that of the westerners. Obviously, it gets

Table 5.1

Monthly housing rent paid by the Immigrant Nationals in Kuwait (KD) Kuwait-Dinar

	Less than KD 30	*30*	*50*	*70*	*90*	*110*	*150*	*190*	*230*	Average
1. Palestinians & Jordanians	1.4	24.4	30.9	17.4	8.8	9.1	5.1	1.9	1.0	78.2
2. Arabs from Arabian Gulf	13.1	13.1	8.7	8.7	17.4	4.3	30.4	-	4.3	105.0
3. Egyptians	1.5	4.6	23.9	21.4	13.3	23.0	8.2	3.6	0.5	99.4
4. Other Arabs	1.0	15.6	25.8	19.0	11.2	12.7	9.8	2.0	2.9	92.9
5. Indians	-	2.1	12.5	12.5	12.5	22.9	29.1	6.3	2.1	128.5
6. Pakistanis	15.8	10.5	26.3	15.8	-	15.8	10.5	5.3	-	85.3
7. Other Asians	5.3	10.5	15.8	21.0	15.8	5.3	10.5	15.8	-	105.4
8. Others	-	16.7	-	-	16.7	33.3	-	-	33.3	150.0

Source: Sample Survey - A1-moosa (1981).

Table 5.2

Housing density of Immigrant labour force in Kuwait - per person per room (%)

Person in one room	*Less than 1 room*	*1*	*2*	*3*	*4*	*5*	*6*	*7 and above*	*Average*
1. Palestinians & Jordanians	4.7	29.0	36.3	18.6	8.1	1.8	1.0	0.5	2.6
2. Arabs from Arabian Gulf	12.0	36.0	12.0	8.0	4.1	8.0	-	-	2.1
3. Egyptians	7.6	55.5	29.7	4.4	2.0	0.4	0.4	-	1.9
4. Other Arabs	9.8	42.1	29.9	9.4	5.8	0.4	0.4	0.4	2.2
5. Indians	17.3	63.5	19.2	-	-	-	-	-	1.5
6. Pakistanis	4.0	50.0	20.0	12.0	4.0	-	-	-	2.02
7. Other Asians	4.5	40.9	27.3	9.1	9.1	-	-	-	2.5
8. Others	71.4	19.0	4.8	4.8	-	-	-	-	0.93

Source: Sample Survey - A1-moosa (1981).

to an understanding that the Indian community is the second leading community in income, housing, living conditions, the Europeans and Americans are however well placed, basically due to their executive positions and attractive wages and concessions.

Housing Conditions of the Hyderabadi Workers Repatriated from Kuwait

The housing conditions of the repatriated Hyderabadi workers from Kuwait has been satisfactory. The foremost objective of the migrants was to invest a major part of their savings towards housing. Most of those who already owned a house had plans for renovation or reconstruction. Those who were staying in the rented house were in search of a already built house, or have purchased a plot and constructed a house.

The Hyderabadi workers realized the significance of real estate and were in a continuous process to acquire one. The increasing demand for land and house and the capacity of the migrants to pay a maximum created a big housing market. Numerous Agencies established to assist and direct, purchase of plots and houses. The large number of multi-storeyed residential and commercial complexes appeared all over Hyderabad at centrally located places. The migrants also ventured to purchase a number of plots or sometimes in acres of land at the city outskirts. This they did speculating future prospects.

The enormous competition and filling up of vacant lands was conspicuous in the whole of Hyderabad. Obviously the people who did not migrate had to face a strong challenge, for the latter were not in a position to pay in excess, the migrants had more money and lesser stay in Hyderabad. Hence, they purchased whatever they found is saleable. For they thought this is the only field of investment. The immobile property shall always be useful in case of their return or at least for their younger generations.

Another problem aroused due to the migrants purchase of lands outside the city was kept vacant for decades. Having registered they had the option to either build a house or sale the plot, they did neither, but kept the plots for higher demand with passage of time. This situation still added to the problems of those Hyderabadis who at least wanted to leave the inner city and move over to periphery. Hence, the housing conditions in Hyderabad needs to be analysed keeping the above constraints given above in mind.

House

The opportunes of migration provided the local population of the Hyderabad an earnest substantial income from abroad. This has enabled saving of surplus money. Hence investment became inevitable. The housing conditions of these people before migration were not satisfactory due to their low economic profile, subsistence income, excess of expenditure heavy indebtedness hindered developmental activities particularly renovation, relocation, new construction of Houses was a difficult task. Congestion, dilapidation prevailed which often created discomfort to the house-hold members and to the guests visiting. Joint family system added to the difficulties of congestion of housing accommodation.

House-hold Size

The presence of large joint families in Hyderabad, particularly of the Muslim house-holds becomes a significant variable in housing analysis. The large Muslim families is the result of fundamentalism, sentimentalism, lack of practicing birth control, high fertility of Muslim women etc. Since, a large number of the male members of the house-hold emigrated abroad since 1970s, a certain change in these families is noticed particularly in the size of the house-hold.

The average house-hold size of Hyderabad city given by the 1981 census is 6 members, and the inner city had 7 members. The house-hold of the Hyderabadi workers repatriated from Kuwait has shown 4.8 members before and 4.7 members after migration. However the technicians and drivers house-hold size remained above average. The house-hold size of the drivers families remained above 6 members before and after migration. This is because, most of the drivers migrated were middle aged and were already having sufficient children. (see Table 5.3).

Investment on Housing

The plight of persons who owned houses and the rented people was alike and acute. Owned house-holders were sometimes struggling for more space and in a few cases there was sufficient vacant land but lack of finance, restricted building activity.

The problems of the rented house members was serious that they were facing, low sanitation, poor drainage, shortage of drinking water in addition to the suppression of the owners: restricting in every action of the rentiers. The higher demand of rent had its own problem. Almost every year a new issue is triggered between the owners and rentiers. This type of situation is universal. However, the Muslim community tenureship is unique. This is largely due to illiteracy, poverty, low income, large families.

Table 5.3

Average House-hold size of the Hyderabadi workers repatriated from Kuwait (occupation-wise)

	Average House-hold workers before migration	*Average House-hold workers after migration*
1. Professionals	3.7	2.9
2. Technical	5.2	5.7
3. Service workers	3.5	3.6
4. Drivers	6.4	6.1
Total	4.8	4.7

Source: Sample Survey - Hyderabad (1991).

Once, the migrants return with certain savings, the foremost concern was to renovate their houses. Despite several constraints, priorities and other obligations the migrants paid special attention to their immediate housing needs. Several years of struggle in the old house the migrants first priority was housing. Hence it is observed irrespective of the scaling every migrant did invest either on renovation, reconstruction or new house construction both for dwelling and rental purposes in Hyderabad (see Table 5.4).

Occupational category-wise migrants invested to various tunes of amount is listed in the above table. The range is as less as fifty thousand to five lakh rupees. However no separate analysis is made on renovation, repairs, or construction. The amount invested on housing after migration is ranged and recorded for the present study and analysis.

Above fifty per cent of the professionals have invested to a tune of three lakhs and the rest upto five lakhs and above. Maximum investment of the tecnicians went upto three lakhs, servicians upto five lakhs, drivers spent arount two lakhs on housing.

Seventy per cent of the technicians spent about two lakh rupees and thirty per cent upto three lakh rupees. Fifty per cent each of the servicians invested two lakh rupees and five lakh rupees respectively. The category of drivers sixty per cent of them invested upto one lakh and the rest upto two lakh rupees.

The trend and the magnitude of amount expended on housing by the workers goes *vis-a-vis* to their profession and income. This is very well reflected by the table. Besides, the duration of stay in Kuwait also played a key role on the saving and investment amount and the location of housing in the city. The intra city residential mobility has shown that people moved from dilapitated zones to city rich sophisticated zones.

The overall investment pattern reveals that fifty-five per cent of all the categories have invested as much as two lakhs and the rest spent beyond five lakh rupees. It is observed that low investment in most of the cases is spent for only repairs and renovation. The higher expenditure was basically and significantly for the purpose of new housing constructions. As already mentioned the duration of stay in Kuwait of the migrants reflects on the better economic and capability of more investment on Housing. It is also observed that the migrants before lived in a bad housing conditions. This eventually resulted for the migrants to immediately concentrate on housing development.

It is also observed that the professional migrants and others who stayed a long in Kuwait built new houses but not rented them. This is due to fear that the rentiers would not easily vacate or that they may occupy permanently and illegally or they may damage the building are a few causes. In the absence of the migrant rented people can misuse the houses by sublet also is a matter of concern with the owners. Hence, they made it clear that only their own confidential people occupy the house with no rent. They did not care for the meager expected rent. Since their own income was more than enough to get a smooth life than the speculated legal issues and risks involved in leaving their houses on rent.

The lower category personnel had a positive view on building activity, they were anxious to let their houses or sublet also if necessary. This was due to the limited income and more expenditure.

Table 5.4

Average amount invested on Housing (Occupation-wise) Hyderabadi workers repatriated from Kuwait

Amount in Rs./ Occupation	*Below 50,000*	*50,001 1,00,000*	*1,00,001 1,50,000*	*1,50,001 2,00,000*	*2,00,001 3,00,000*	*3,00,001 5,00,000*	*Above 5,00,000*
1. Professionals	-	-	-	5.9	47.1	23.5	23.5
2. Technicians	-	25.0	18.8	25.0	31.2	-	-
3. Service	-	11.8	11.8	27.8	35.3	11.8	-
4. Drivers	16.7	44.4	16.7	22.2	-	-	-
Total	4.4	14.7	11.8	26.5	27.9	11.8	5.9

Source: Sample Survey - Hyderabad (1991).

Hence, it is seen that drivers and technicians were particular to commercialize their houses or preferably construct shopping portions or and also purchase already existing shops or purchase land on the road side to commercialize in future. Hence, varieties of plans were made to gain more rent and establish sufficient income after their return to Hyderabad permanently.

Monthly earnings of the migrants has a positive impact on the amount of investment. Hence attempt is made to highlight average income-wise investment of the house-holds on housing (see Table 5.5).

Income-wise it is observed that twenty-nine per cent of the house-holds with less than ten thousand rupees of monthly income invested in an average of 0.43 lakh rupees. Those earning upto twenty lakh rupees per month 43% of such house-holds invested 0.93 lakh rupees. And seventy per cent of the house-holds earning upto thirty thousand rupees per month spent as much as 2.8 lakh rupees. Ninety per cent of earners upto fifty thousand rupees invested 4.8 lakh rupees, lastly 100% of the people earning above fifty thousand rupees per month have spent above 6.6 lakh rupees. A significant observation is lower the income lower the investment is clearly depicted in the table. The income and investment are directly proportional as regards to the investment on housing needs of the migrants in Hyderabad.

Table 5.5

Average Investment on Housing - Hyderabadi workers repatriated from Kuwait (Income-wise)

Monthly Income in Rupees	*Per cent House-holds Investment*	*Average Investment in lakhs of rupees*
Below - 10,000	29.0	0.43
10,001 - 20,000	43.0	0.93
20,001 - 30,000	70.0	2.8
30,001 - 50,000	90.9	4.8
Above - 50,000	100.0	6.6

Source: Sample Survey - Hyderabad - 1991.

The demand of the construction material, the vacant land/plot the site/situation all underwent a remarkable transformation and demand ever since 1970's in the city. Vijaya Bhole (1988) observed vacant land by city zones of Hyderabad as 2.6% and 51.8% and 45.6% for Hyderabad South, North and Secunderabad respectively. There is clear evidence that Hyderabad North and areas of Secunderabad provided much vacant lands for new residential colonies. South of Hyderabad was depleted of vacant land and presently, only vertical development is possible. Even otherwise, the South of Hyderabad is developed beyond its city limits with majority of the migrants from all over the state of Andhra Pradesh concentrated on the National Highway No. 9. New colonies cropped up and the development is still on. It is these parts in the South of Hyderabad and towards south-east where the "Barkas" area an old Arab locality where maximum people migrated and invested large amounts on housing activities are conspicuous.

Housing Conditions : Owned : Income-wise

The structure of the house with regards to its scale of standardisation, built and strength of the building is divided into pucca, semi-pucca and kaccha condition, each term has some limitation, specification as per the census of India. However individual researcher can have a choice of his own scale as per his comfort.

The structural conditions of housing of all the migrants before was that it was seventy to eighty per cent of earners below rupees three thousand of income per month lived in dilapidated kaccha houses. Persons earning above this income had pucca structures. It is also found that the migrants had lot of housing problems, they could not repair or maintain better houses due to their low income, expenditure and house-hold size were the haunted liabilities. They were struggling to upgrade their housing conditions. They could not venture a new residence change for fear of various repercussions. It was wise to carry on with the existing conditions hence nobody ventured to move away from their old buildings.

After migration with sufficient financial resources, majority of the migrants first preferred to renovate their abodes. It was necessary in terms of security as they had already acquired costly assets like Gold, Electronic equipment, and other items which required a better house besides a social position in the society (see Tables 5.6 & 5.7).

Table 5.6

Housing condition - Owned - Hyderabadi workers before migration to Kuwait (Income-wise)

Monthly Income in Rupees	*Pucca*	*Semi-Pucca*	*Kaccha*	*Average area in Sq.Yds.*	*Average No. of Rooms*
Less than 1,000	7.2	9.5	83.3	96.0	1.6
1,001 - 2,000	17.0	12.8	70.2	53.0	2.3
2,001 - 3,000	15.8	21.0	70.2	99.0	2.6
3,001 - 4,000	100.0	-	-	204.0	3.0
Above - 5,000	100.0	-	-	315.0	4.0
Total	16.1	12.5	71.4	83.4	2.7

Source: Sample Survey - Hyderabad - 1991.

Table 5.7

Housing condition - Owned - Hyderabadi workers repatriated from Kuwait (Income-wise)

Monthly Income in Rupees	*Pucca*	*Semi-Pucca*	*Kaccha*	*Average Area in Sq.Yds*	*Average No. of Rooms*
Less than 10,000	47.6	44.0	8.0	122.0	3.6
10,001 - 20,000	60.0	35.0	5.0	197.0	4.2
20,001 - 30,000	85.7	14.0	0.3	290.0	4.8
30,001 - 50,000	100.0	-	-	324.0	5.0
Above - 50,000	100.0	-	-	362.0	5.7
Total	64.4	26.8	9.8	182.7	4.7

Source: Sample Survey - Hyderabad - 1991.

The income-wise trend of the structure of the building the average area and the rooms in each house-hold has changed significantly. Almost reverse conditions prevailed before to after migration. Fifty per cent to cent per cent after migrants lived in pucca houses hitherto this was in connivance to their amount of monthly income.

The semi-pucca and kaccha housing conditions decreased drastically with the increase in income.

Significant change has been observed in the area and number of rooms. Once again, this exhibited the ascending order with ascending income. It is quite true that the change in economic position brings revolution in social and economic pursuits. The migrants first emphasis and importance after migration was housing, this was not only for dwelling but as a guarantee of income generation in case of their total return. Hence, irrespective of the income few but all regarded better housing as the most significant and vital need and necessity.

The concept of "multiple deprivation" of the inner city was observed by Ratna Naidu "Inner city of Hyderabad" (1986). In the inner city dilapidation and blight is rooted in what is technically known in the literature as the phenomena of "multiple deprivation". Multiple deprivation is a series of correlated cross cutting deprivations which often compound one another. In the social science literature this vicious cycle of multiple deprivation, of, for instance, poor education and training, low income, poor diet, low hygienic condition leading to low efficiency and low ability for getting enhanced income is analytically applied to understand poverty at the individual community and class levels. This is the classic "interlocking series of deprivation". However the concept of multiple deprivation in the inner city should be applied (as is more usual in urban studies) on an area basis. Due to some historical and cultural factors the inner city area was deprived of the developmental impulses which propel the metropolis.

Deprived of economic opportunities with the dismantling of feudal structure and deprived of its elite, who are usually the powerful spokesmen for the enhancement of civic amenities, the inner city as an area languishes from multiple deprivations. To the economic and civic deprivations, must also be added the deprivation which accrues from the alienation of the communities from each other resulting in frequent communal riots. Thus it is found that the inner city the classic syndrome where the different types of deprivations mesh into one another, to create, for those who must endure them, a total situation shot through and through by one level of deprivation after another.

Hence, the variation of deprivations the housing conditions also show a variety of class. The city of Hyderabad and its housing condition can be accrued of the civic and economic, educational deprivations which resulted not only strikingly in the poverty but reflects on their housing conditions. Often rifts between the owners and tenants are the results of lack of amenities and facilities and the ever deterioting and dilapidation of the housing structure. A large amount of investment on housing in Hyderabad can be attributed to the "syndrome of multiple deprivations" concept.

The housing conditions of the walled city in the year 1951 was 35.94% Pucca and 64.07% Kaccha. But by the passing of three decades in the year 1981 it reversed. There were 64.21% Pucca houses and 35.77% Kaccha houses Ratna Naidu (1986). She also showed that Muslims lived 45.28% in Kaccha structures 18.61% in Pucca and 36.21% lived in Kaccha-Pucca houses.

It is found in case of the Kuwaiti repatriates that 42.9 per cent possessed their own houses before migration. After migration 72.3 per cent of them had their own houses. This shows that within a span of an average decade stay abroad about thirty per cent of the repatriates possessed their own houses, which indicates that the majority of these were investing in housing and that they were saving as much as they could purchase a house or construct one in future. The economic potential is established by the about fact of the migrants of Hyderabad to various Gulf countries.

Housing Conditions : Owned : Occupation-wise

The housing conditions of the repatriates before migration to Kuwait as per categories of occupation, details that above fifty-six per cent of all these people had their own pucca houses (not necessarily constructed or purchased by them, but have acquired as ancestral property). The drivers about 10 per cent of them had their houses before migration. The other groups had houses above average.

Categorically we observe that after migration as much as eighty-four per cent of the repatriates had their own houses. Besides the professionals and the servicians covered under the survey revealed cent per cent living in pucca owned houses. The percentage increased to a tune of forty per cent before and after migration in case of service and drivers category and it is seen a change of twenty per cent in the categories of professionals and technicians.

The general increase of about twenty-eight per cent change occurred before and after migration pucca owned housing condition. Two categories are above this average and another two categories of personnel had below this average general growth of pucca owned houses.

The total semi-pucca owned houses average after migration was only twelve per cent and only about four per cent lived in kaccha houses as against twenty nine and fourteen per cent before migration respectively. It is also revealed before migration technicians and servicians were having values close to average, professionals were largely below this average and the drivers were twenty per cent ahead of this average.

The average area possessed by the owned housed repatriates added to around fifty sq. yards. Additional one room was possessed before to after migration. This is also a substantial progress in their real estate values.

As already mentioned majority of the house owners had ancestral property and the repatriates have contributed for the renovation. Those who were living in the rented houses afforded to either purchase a readymade house in their choicest locality or elsewhere they purchased plots and constructed new houses. A large number of them purchased additional plots for the purpose of resale and to commercialize (see Tables 5.8 and 5.9).

Table 5.8

Housing condition - Owned - Hyderabadi workers before migration to Kuwait (occupation-wise)

Occupation	*Pucca*	*Semi-Pucca*	*Kaccha*	*Average Area in Sq-Yds.*	*Average No. of Rooms*
Professionals	78.6	14.3	7.1	216.0	2.3
Technicians	60.0	30.0	10.0	170.0	3.1
Service workers	64.7	28.6	7.1	232.0	2.1
Drivers	10.0	50.0	40.0	125.0	2.3
Total	56.2	29.2	14.6	192.4	2.3

Source: Sample Survey - Hyderabad - 1991.

Table 5.9

Housing condition - Owned - Hyderabadi workers repatriated from Kuwait (occupation-wise)

Occupation	*Pucca*	*Semi-Pucca*	*Kaccha*	*Average Area in Sq-Yds.*	*Average No. of Rooms*
Professionals	100.0	-	-	293.0	4.3
Technicians	78.9	21.1	-	186.0	3.5
Service workers	100.0	-	-	305.0	3.2
Drivers	52.6	31.6	15.8	188.0	2.5
Total	83.9	12.2	3.8	246.6	3.4

Source: Sample Survey - Hyderabad - 1991.

Housing Conditions (Rented) Occupation-wise

The ever growing demand of housing the floating population to city and the economic capability of the repatriates to opt better quality house, locality and with all civic amenities and facilities in many a cases resulted in a demand for flat system in the twin cities. Annual contract rental deeds with advance annual payment are common all over the city. In order to contain the litigation crisis the owners restrict the rental duration to a limited period. Thereupon they stress to vacate. The rentiers unable to keep on shifting from place to place and locality to locality immediately agree for extra rent, annual advance etc. If however things are not sorted out, the rentier is left with the option or pleading with the rent control authorities, so the litigation commences resulting to worst situations.

Given the plight of the owners and renters, the repatriates always attempt to escape the "rent demon" and wish to have a small house of their own. In case they cannot afford, they, insist for a better quality rental accommodation and preferably a locality which is secure and safe from communal tensions and a house where the owners does not reside, but, it is a independent house.

The social ethos of the Muslim repatriates of the city has contained their living closer to their community. The ideas and actions of one community are always different from the other. The growth of children in close accordance to community principles and religious options stress and strain the people to adjust within the community environment and sphere. The muslim house-wife being confined in the house prefers social association with her close kith and kin and others of her own taste and category. Hence the choice of a rental accommodation depends on the basis of security, accessibility and cultural, affinity and that the amount of rent is not a concern for the repatriates.

The Kuwaiti repatriates in Hyderabad have shown that before their migration 57 per cent lived in rented houses and it came down to 27.7 per cent after migration. This decrease of rental houses denotes that the repatriates firstly became economically potential to own houses, secondly, to overcome the litigations and constant pestering of owners forced them to own a house of any stature till they construct one of their own.

The occupational category-wise data reveals before migration only twenty-five per cent had pucca houses. This value is exactly to that of the drivers per centage, only 15 per cent technicians had pucca houses the professionals and the servicians had above the average values. The after migration revealed forty-five per cent afforded to live in pucca houses. Except technicians (27.3%) all other categories of people had above the total average values.

The low percentage of technicians in pucca houses and maximum in semi-pucca houses is only because the technicians required a shop/residence at one location. Since the duration of work and other aspects made them convenient to have both activities at one place. That is why the technicians have lesser pucca houses.

The semi-pucca housing condition before migration for all the categories was (57.8%) and it declined to (41.9%). It is found as mentioned above eighty per cent of the technicians lived in semi-pucca structure before migration and yet (72.2%) stayed back in the same structure after migration. Since the technicians lived in Kuwait with a feeling that they would come back soon to city and establish their old activities. Hence they opted not to vacate their old house for future speculation.

It is also observed that the professionals retained the same before and after migration (50%). A big change is noticed in the occupance of the servicians and drivers (see Tables 5.10 and 5.11).

Table 5.10

Housing condition - Rented - Hyderabadi workers before migration to Kuwait (occupation-wise)

Occupation	*Pucca*	*Semi-Pucca*	*Kaccha*	*Average Area in Sq-Yds.*	*Average No. of Rooms*	*Monthly Rent in Paid Rupees*
Professionals	37.5	50.0	12.5	168.0	2.5	300
Technicians	15.0	80.0	5.0	174.0	3.4	320
Service workers	31.0	43.0	26.0	126.0	3.1	248
Drivers	25.0	50.0	25.0	90.0	2.8	120
Total	25.0	57.8	17.2	134.3	2.9	234

Source: Sample Survey - Hyderabad - 1981.

Table 5.11

Housing condition - Rented - Hyderabadi workers repatriated from Kuwait (occupation-wise)

Occupation	*Pucca*	*Semi-Pucca*	*Kaccha*	*Average Area in Sq-yds*	*Average No. of Rooms*	*Monthly Rent Paid in Rs.*
Professionals	50.0	50.0	-	125.0	3.0	300
Technicians	27.3	72.7	-	115.0	3.9	430
Service workers	57.2	28.6	14.2	157.0	4.2	456
Drivers	54.5	18.2	27.3	105.0	3.5	570
Total	45.2	41.9	12.9	120.3	3.6	476

Source: Sample Survey - Hyderabad - 1991.

The kaccha housing condition of the rentiers revealed 17 per cent and 13 per cent before to after migration respectively. But the complete absence of professionals and technicians in the kaccha houses after migration is expected. The drivers category did not show a big change, but the servicians have shifted to semi-pucca houses from kaccha considerably before to after migration.

The Average area in square yards occupied in the rental houses of the repatriates before to after migration has gone down, but at the same time the average number of rooms and the amount of rent paid increased considerably. The lesser area, of the two occupational categories is explained for the fact that there was change of house, locality and with an extra room. The rent almost doubled is due to shift in a new house and the ability of the repatriates to pay more rent.

Housing Condition (Rented) Income-Wise

In order to understand the structure of rent paid structure according to the income of the repatriates, separate tables with information pertaining to before and after migration are prepared. It is seen that repatriates, before migration, earning upto Rs. 3000 per month, 25 per cent of them lived in pucca houses. 37.5 per cent each lived in semi-pucca and kaccha structures. After migration with the immense increase in the income about 74.2 per cent lived in pucca house 22.6 per cent lived in semi-pucca and only 3.2 per cent lived in kaccha houses. About 3/4 of the repatriates staying in pucca rented houses and paying an average rent of Rs. 490 per month after migration reflects that a majority of them preferred to occupy pucca houses, since there were a large number of new pucca houses being built by their own friends or relatives staying abroad, this enabled the repatriates easy availability of pucca houses. A minimum of them are still living in kaccha house after migration. This appears due to the house-holders may be the recent migrants and that they would shift the house early in the near future (see Tables 5.12 and 5.13).

Internal Territorial Residential Scheme of Repatriates

Geographers based on territorial scheme have evolved five perspectives of migrants. Firstly, change of residence from one parish or commune to another (Hagersta, 1957). Secondly, change of residence as a symbol of transition from one surrounding to another in the course of human life (Weinberg 1961), thirdly, physical transition also leads to abandoning of one social setting and entering into another and different one (Eisenstadt 1953). Fourthly migration is a form of motivated behaviour. It takes place through the volition of individuals or families concerned (Thomas 1954). Fifthly and lastly, migration as an act of volition implies decision-making based on some criteria, which usually involve a hierarchy of values (Mangalam 1968).

Table 5.12

Housing condition - Rented - Hyderabadi workers before migration to Kuwait (Income-wise)

Occupation	*Pucca*	*Semi-Pucca*	*Kaccha*	*Average Area in Sq-Yds.*	*Average No. of Rooms*	*Monthly Rent Paid in Rs.*
Below 1000	13.6	36.4	50.0	107.0	2.0	215
1001-2000	24.1	41.4	34.5	126.0	2.3	280
2001-3000	46.2	30.8	23.0	127.0	2.2	407
Total	25.0	37.5	37.5	119.0	2.1	284

Source: Sample Survey - Hyderabad - 1991.

Table 5.13

Housing condition - Rented - Hyderabadi workers repatriated from Kuwait (Income-wise)

Occupation	*Pucca*	*Semi-Pucca*	*Kaccha*	*Average Area in Sq-Yds.*	*Average No. of Rooms*	*Monthly Rent Paid in Rs.*
Below 10,000	70.4	25.9	3.7	138.0	2.8	345
10,001-20,000	100	-	-	122.0	2.5	548
20,001-30,000	100	-	-	130.0	2.3	815
Total	74.2	22.6	3.2	124.4	2.5	490

Source: Sample Survey - Hyderabad - 1991.

The above five perspectives are summed up as "Migration, is a relatively permanent moving away of a collectivity, called migrants, from one geographical location to another, preceded by decision-making on the part of the migrants on the basis of a hierarchically ordered set of values or valued ends and resulting in changes in the interactional system of the migrants" (Mangalam 1968).

Mobility includes all kinds of temporary and permanent territorial movement over various distances, migration relates to a permanent change of residence. However, Zelinsky urged that such a distinction should not be over emphasized, he observed : "Genuine migration obviously means the perceptible and simultaneous shifts in both spatial and social locus, so that the student cannot realistically measure one kind of movement while he ignores the other - Ideally, we should observe shifts in both varieties of space in tandem but given the dearth of techniques and data for handling purely social movement, we are forced to rely solely on territorial movements as a clumsy surrogate for total mobility" (Zelinsky 1971).

The internal residential territorial scheme of Hyderabad was studied by Bhole Vijaya (1988) she implied that the inner city residential growth and development has five determinates viz physical, demographic, politico historical socio/cultural and economic. The residential land use in the urban fringe of Hyderabad is classified as demographic, economic, legal and other.

For the present study the socio/cultural and economic determinants in the inner city contributed by the repatriates transformed the physical and demographic change to a very large extent. The residential re-location of repatriates within the city and much more in the urban fringe is highlighted.

Large number of muslim repatriates with a sense of communal and economic insecurity preferred to move towards the peripheral parts of the city. Their determination of maintaining a strong cultural and social bondage with the community remained intact A good network of transport routes and roads supported their motive, besides the capability of owing transport vehicles also assured their link with the area of origin to areas of destination within the city in the form of daily commuting between old and new cultural environs.

Social Area of Hyderabad Metropolis and Distribution of Hyderabadi Kuwaitis

A pioneer work on identifying the social area of Hyderabad metropolis was made by Manzoor Alam (1972). He divided metropolitan Hyderabad into four social area zones viz. (1). Areas of Social Escalation (ESC), (2). Areas of Economic Transition (ET), (3). Areas of Social Transition (ST) and (4). Areas of Social Depression (DEP). The basis of such zones was the level of literacy, concentration or dispersion of economic activities. Further he divided Historically Hyderabad into three units-Hyderabad South, North and Secunderabad.

A recent study by Rao (1990) was made to identity the social ecology of the metropolitan Hyderabad. Factor analysis technique was used. Four main groups - social, economic, demographic and physical congestion using twenty-three variables, the metropolis was mapped to delineate zones viz. very high, high, medium and low social ecology.

The zone of very high social ecology included the CBD of the metropolis comprising the central core commercial areas of Abids, Koti, Sultan Bazar, Troop Bazar, Esamia Bazar, another high elite residential zone of Banjara Hills, Journalist Colony, Salarjung Colony etc. were listed. Obviously the commercial areas and the elite residential area consist of sprawling socio-economic amenities and facilities, hence the zone has very rich civic amenities. Heavy building structures and more organized and planned transport system. In general this area had covered two wards viz. four and eight of the city. The former is located in the centre of the city and the latter on the north east fringe.

The second zone of high social ecology included wards viz. one, three, seven, fifteen and sixteen. These are fairly rich residential zones. Ward one is attached to Secunderabad South area, ward three and fifteen are attached on the North East and west of the commercial core of the city, as such they are influenced by the core neighbourhood. Ward seven is North East of the eighth ward mainly covering the rich residential zone of Banjara Hill. Ameerpet, Sanjeevreddy Nagar and the oldest industrial area of the city of the Sanathnagar and Erragadda include this ward. Hence, it is observed that these high social zones are the neighbours and spatially contiguous areas to the very high social ecology zones of the metropolis.

The third zone of medium character comprised by half of the city wards. These includes all types of residential, and commercial areas of the city which exhibit a medium character in all the ways. This zone is stretched from east to west of the city including old colonies, peripheries with large number or migrants. The area is spread both north and south of the Musi river.

Lastly the fourth zone is the urban and commercial decay zone, mainly located extreme south of the city with very old dilapidated houses, poor transport, unorganized building structures, meager civic amenities is characterised by this area.

Residential Mobility

The intra urban re-distribution and migration of the house-hold and the changing urban residential pattern 19 associated with a number of variables. The intra-urban mobility is the direct result of the change in the socio-economic conditions ethic and cultural segregation, politibing housing and planning. The dynamic concept of urban spatial structure is the result of intra urban changes and movement.

The decision-making of the residential change, generally within the given city is related to family needs, security, better housing, improved infrastructure. Various scholars studied the residential mobility. Julian Wolpert (1970) viewed mobility as an adaptation to the perceived change in the surroundings, field theory approach to search behaviour which relates to movers source of informations about his action space and the life cycle stage.

Turner J. (1976) mentioned the residential mobility is the result of a "trade off" between three factors, tenure status, location and housing and space needs. The economic factor of income as a major constraints in the nature of housing and residential mobility is presented by various scholars like Ball and Kirwan (1976), Bourne and Hitchoch (1978), Basset and Short (1980).

Vijaya (1988) studied the residential mobility of Hyderabad. She observed the positive factors are the socio-economic conditions and the negative factors "induced mobility forces" due to stress and strain. She concluded in Hyderabad the residential mobility is characterised by short distance moves. There is a tendency to relocate nearer to the point of origin producing a circular migration field. Income, culture and ethnicity distort migration field along a sectoral axis and finally suburbanisation is not due to extension of migration field of higher income groups from the central city.

The residential mobility of the Hyderabadi workers repatriated from Kuwait essentially is an induced phenomenon of substantial income change, security due to communal tensions, availability of vacant land in the suburbs preferably in the south and south west of Hyderabad. The residential mobility is also associated with movement from underprivileged social areas of the city to a better and sophisticated city zones. A large number of migrants to middle east in Hyderabad transformed their existing environment from worst to the best. This is evident from the new housing structure, multi-storeyed buildings and improved infra-structural facilities.

Location of Owned Residential Houses : Occupation-wise - Social Area-wise

An attempt is made to trace the new location of owned houses of the repatriates prior and in post migration phases. It is observed that the socially high zones retained intact the same houses before and after migration. There were 66.5%, 2.1% and 8.4%, owned houses located in very high medium and low social zones before migration. The socially low zones and very high zones respectively show increased values after migration, whereas the medium zone a low value. This re-allocation, redistribution is understood of the fact that the low social zones have cheap land open and secure areas. The people have set-up organized colonies in the vacant lands with more residential area and a calm atmosphere to live. The very high increase is attributed to the fact that the owners largely went for multi-storeyed apartments. It can be assumed that low social area acquired horizontal and very high social areas acquired vertical growth of the housing.

Occupation-wise, the owned house personnel, we find ten per cent servicians and two per cent drivers and none of the professionals or technicians before migration are in the very high social core. After migration, five per cent technicians and drivers intruded in this zone. Similarly the high rented social area had twenty-three per cent added of the repatriates. However servicians and drivers five per cent of each of them moved towards low zones. The medium zone has experienced substantial decrease of technicians and drivers after post migration. Lastly the low social areas registered that all the categories of people five per cent of them got accommodated in this area (see Tables 5.14 and 5.15).

Location of Residential Houses : Income-wise - Social Area-wise

The average monthly income of the people directly asserts the capacity and capability of the repatriates to own a house and also reflects the social zone in which they would seek accommodation. Hence an attempt is made to study the income-wise location of owned residences and their mobility elsewhere before and after migration.

A glance at both the tables reveals that there is an overall increase in the three zones, very high, high and low before and after migration. But a significant decrease in the medium zones is observed. This is due to most of the people in addition to an own house opted another owned house elsewhere in the city, and for the purpose of security and readjustment in the society moved in different directions of the city (see Tables 5.16 and 5.17).

Table 5.14

Social Area-wise location of Owned Residential Houses — Hyderabadi workers before migration to Kuwait

Sl. No.	*Occupation*	*Very High*	*High*	*Medium*	*Low*	*Total*
1.	Professionals	-	14.2	85.8	-	100
2.	Technicians	-	20.1	69.9	10.0	100
3.	Service and others	10.0	35.6	54.4	-	100
4.	Drivers	2.1	20.0	47.9	30.0	100
	Total	2.1	23.0	66.5	8.4	100

Source: Sample Survey - Hyderabad - 1991.

Table 5.15

Social Area-wise locations of Owned Residential Houses — Hyderabadi workers repatriated from Kuwait

Sl. No.	*Occupation*	*Very High*	*High*	*Medium*	*Low*	*Total*
1.	Professionals	-	15.0	80.0	5.0	100
2.	Technicians	5.3	21.2	42.4	15.9	100
3.	Service and others	8.6	30.1	57.0	4.3	100
4.	Drivers	5.3	26.5	36.4	31.8	100
	Total	4.6	23.1	59.1	13.2	100

Source: Sample Survey - Hyderabad - 1991.

Table 5.16

Social Area-wise location of Owned Residential Houses (Income-wise)

Income in Rupees	*Very High*	*High*	*Medium*	*Low*	*Total*
< 500	-	11.1	88.9	-	100.0
501-1,000	5.9	23.7	70.4	-	100.0
1,001-2,000	7.1	21.3	64.5	7.1	100.0
2,001-3,000	-	20.0	40.0	40.0	100.0
3,001-5,000	-	33.3	66.7	-	100.0
Total	4.2	21.0	64.3	10.5	100.0

Source: Sample Survey - Hyderabad - 1991.

Table 5.17

Social Area-wise concentration of Owned Residential Hyderabadi workers repatriated from Kuwait (Income-wise)

Income in Rupees	*Very High*	*High*	*Medium*	*Low*	*Total*
< 10,000	-	50.0	50.0	-	100.0
10,001-20,000	-	25.2	37.8	12.6	100.0
20,001-30,000	10.4	18.2	56.2	15.2	100.0
30,001-50,000	10.0	20.0	50.0	20.0	100.0
> 50,000	-	33.3	66.7	-	100.0
Total	7.2	25.7	47.3	14.4	100.0

Source: Sample Survey - Hyderabad - 1991.

The income-wise situation shows people earning about Rs. 2000 per month before migration were concentrated in the very high rated social zones of the present day. Also is noticed the high-income groups were conspicuously absent in this zone, but disappearance of the low income group and appearance of high income group prominently signifies that income did have a positive impact on the residential capability of being located in the socially very high rated zones.

Another general trend observed before migration shows a large chunk of people resided in the medium rate zone of all the income groups. After migration there is a feature of redistribution. Mostly people occupied high and low social zones as well along with medium rated zone. This again reflects the fact that the saving capacity of the people or the very high income motivated them to move into high social zones and at times attracted into the low zones. The higher social zones are supposed to elevate a better social environment and discipline. People wanted their children to form a cream of the society by sharing all the services and amenities available to the upper elite groups.

The option of having a house in the low social areas is mainly to invest their surplus savings and derive rent. As the land is cheap and there is no dearth of renters. This encourages people to own a house in such zones. It is also observed in later years the owners feel that they themselves can reside for they find that all the civic amenities are available. It is also safe and secure. Hence, it is note worthy that the lower social zones of the city are being filled by the repatriates and migrants. And it is assumed that in no time that the lower social areas would be transformed as high social zones. The economic potential of the people converts the lower zones to rich localities.

Another general feature of housing in Hyderabad shows most of the free and vacant lands either of Government or "Benami" (nameless) owners is illegally and informally occupied by various community of people. Eventually the localities are named after certain popular leaders and are protected by their followers. Hence, a majority of the repatriates are found to be occupying this cheaper and city centrally located dried water tanks, green fields, old places, Hillocks etc. later they have built very good pucca houses in such places. Since, land was available either free or at a nominal cost. Most of such residences do not possess legal documents of house plan, registration.

Residential segregation of Hyderabad city was studied by Vijaya Bhole (1985) she has observed that religion, and language are core determinants of segregation, income and industrial locations are followed by. The residential segregation appears to have shifted from historic and cultural determinants to socio-cultural, socio-industrial, and presently the city is undergoing socio-economic transformation in terms of residential relocation and redistribution with enormous residential mobility within the city.

Social Area-wise-Location of Rented Residential Areas of the Repatriates : Occupation-wise

The socio-economic transformation of the repatriates tended a lots of house-holds to either have one own house or if cannot own stay in a rented house at any social zone, with pucca and posh accommodation. Absence of owner is the best attracted house for the rentiers. However it is observed the local muslim community has lesser attraction to reside in rich social zones in general, but for the muslim repatriates have a tendency to seek abode in richer social areas either owned if not rented.

Rental accommodation among muslims is not a temporary phenomenon but a permanent one. Always their priorities are something else other than residential location. They never vacate house once occupied, unless driven out through legally and of other anti-social means. Maximum cases in the rent control board have Muslim housed litigations Owners anticipating the trouble, rent their houses on agreement bonds renewable every year and with a constant increase in the rent every year. This obviously keeps the rentiers on rocks and if they cannot satisfy the owners conditions, the only way out is to search for a new house. Hence, the owner and the rentier are always unhappy with one another.

The distribution of rental repatriates before and after migration by occupations category has shown that there is the same percentage in low social area and there is decrease of percentage in all other zones. This shows that the repatriates have lesser attraction for rental accommodation and that they are mostly owning a house after migration in the comparatively city rich zones.

The professionals who were scattered in all the social zones before migration are concentrated only in the medium ranked social zone of the city. The technicians who were rented in all zones before migration show that they are now highly concentrated in the medium ranked social zone. The servicians and drivers have also undergone movement from one zone to another but to a lesser extent.

The majority of repatriates rented in medium zone are the people who have lived for over a long period in such zones. Their association with the locality, and the neighbourhood is quite old, and that they have socially and culturally adjusted to this zone and never attempt to be shifted elsewhere. Since medium ranked zone is for the middle class people and it has a right place for the rich ones and the poor ones. The city itself has one half of the area covered under medium ranked social zone. Naturally, people for want of cultural association, social amenities and facilities, accessibility, and with a strong cobweb of friends, relatives are intimately inter twined in such zones. Unlike the high and very high social areas where people do not even know their own neighbours, contram to this, the people of medium zones maintain good social/cultural/economic profiles with one another. There is a tendency and strong bondage and binding in the socially low zones. Every house-hold with particulars of the members, their activities are aware of each other to their fullest knowledge (see Tables 5.18 and 5.19).

Table 5.18

Social Area-wise concentration of Rented Houses - Hyderabadi workers before migration to Kuwait (Occupation-wise)

Sl. No.	*Occupation*	*Very High*	*High*	*Medium*	*Low*	*Total*
1.	Professionals	-	25.0	50.0	25.0	100
2.	Technicians	15.0	35.0	31.1	18.9	100
3.	Service and others	-	6.3	74.8	18.9	100
4.	Drivers	-	20.0	60.0	20.0	100
	Total	6.4	21.9	49.5	22.2	100

Source: Sample Survey - Hyderabad - 1991.

Social Area-wise - Location of Rented Residential Areas of the Repatriates : Income-wise

A study of repatriate rentiers according to their monthly average income before and after migration is also analysed. Conspicuously change of income changed and moulds the condition of living in both negative and positive ways. The very high income of the repatriates brought the economic residential rentier segregation and a considerable change. Increase in percentage in all social zones, except the low social zones. One half of the house-holders before migration from low social zones have disappeared after migration. They got moved into better social areas of the city as their economic capacity of paying more rent has increased (see Tables 5.20 and 5.21).

Table 5.19

Social Area-wise concentration of Rented Houses - Hyderabadi workers repatriated from Kuwait (Occupation-wise)

Sl. No.	*Occupation*	*Very High*	*High*	*Medium*	*Low*	*Total*
1.	Professionals	-	-	100.0	-	100
2.	Technicians	4.1	9.1	72.7	14.1	100
3.	Service and others	-	14.3	71.4	14.3	100
4.	Drivers	-	27.3	63.6	9.1	100
	Total	3.2	16.0	41.6	22.4	100

Source: Sample Survey - Hyderabad - 1991.

Table 5.20

Social Area-wise concentration of Rented Houses - Hyderabadi workers before migration to Kuwait (Income-wise)

Income in Rs.	*Very High*	*High*	*Medium*	*Low*	*Total*
< 500	-	14.2	57.3	28.5	100
501-1000	-	12.5	87.5	-	100
1001-2000	10.5	24.5	56.0	21.0	100
2001-3000	-	46.2	38.4	15.4	100
Total	4.8	25.2	43.4	26.6	100

Source: Sample Survey - Hyderabad - 1991.

Urban Residential Land-use Pattern

The metropolis of Hyderabad has constantly been changing its land-use based on various scores of factors. The inner core was subjected to successive land-use changes. A number of houses located on the road side have been converted to either shops or institutions. Residential land areas succeeded with semi-commercial and residential land use areas to raise income of the house-holds. Subsequently the process of commercialisation is widely spread all over the city. This phenomenon was most prevalent in the densely populated zones of the city. The process also initiated the concept of residence-cum-shop and vertical development of the old houses. The lower ones were meant for shops and the inner and the upper ones for residential rental accommodation.

Table 5.21

Social Area-wise concentration of Rented Houses - Hyderabadi workers repatriated from Kuwait (Income-wise)

Income in Rs.	*Very High*	*High*	*Medium*	*Low*	*Total*
< 20,000	-	-	100.0	-	100
20,001-30,000	7.4	22.8	55.0	14.8	100
30,001-50,000	-	-	100.0	-	100
Total	6.4	28.9	51.9	12.8	100

The poverty stricken Muslim mercantile in the old city could not compete the business exercised by the "Marwaris", eventually a rift between the natives and migrants in terms of social, cultural and economic determinants continued in disguise. The first shock for the Muslim community came when the Nizam surrendered erstwhile Hyderabad state to the Republican India in 1948. A big scale socio-economic and cultural transformation encountered the Hyderabadis. The administrative personnel, military, nobles, ministers all of them have started a different way/style of livelihood. The impact was highly felt by the lower and middle class people.

The reorganization of states and Hyderabad as the capital of Andhra Pradesh in November 1956 once again transformed the intra-urban land-use of the city to a large extent. Many such events had their continued impact on the socio-economic and infrastructure facilities of the city in almost all walks of the life and almost all parts of the city.

The sudden demand of labour in south-west Asian countries for oil exploration created in 1970s came as a very big boon and economic relief for the Muslim population. The unemployed youth were the first to grab and to cling to these opportunities, soon followed by the employed as well. Further these people arranged Visa for their close relatives. Subsequently families started migrated to almost all the countries of south-west Asia.

An important feature prominently observed in the city was that the Muslim community reeling under poverty had only houses of their own as the only assets and some Gold. Studying the migratory process and its economic fruits people ventured either to mortgage or sell out a part or position of their houses for the sake of purchase of Visa, ticket and other expenditure. This allowed the "Marwaris" community who were basically business oriented to exploit the situation to a large extent. By then the muslim community deliberately and knowingly fell prey to this exploitation, hoping that their future shall be better with this change they were not wrong, within no time the male members of the house-hold started sending the petrodollars in thousands of rupees per month. The house-holds who have lost their own houses had also other important things on the list to meet in the first-phase, like female marriages, children's education, purchase of essential and luxury items, grand celebration of feasts, festivals. There are number of cases where the male members migrated come to the economic rescue of their friends, relatives, paid charities, renovation and new construction of mosques and large amounts were given as contributions to the religious and political institutions. The sum total economic change has also reflected in the urban lland-use pattern of the city.

The second phase of expenditure of the Kuwaiti repatriate was on the real estate, purchase of plots, renovation of owned houses, construction of new houses, purchase of flats characterized in this phase. This phase also started to be seized slowly and subsequently. It is in this phase that the residential segregation, particularly that of the repatriates underwent a drastic change. The social zones of the city have encountered a large scale transformation, the general land-use of the city and in particular the residential one has seen a drastic change in the residential pattern of the city.

During the year 1968 the city of Hyderabad had 13.4 residential land-use and about 39% of the vacant land. By the year 1973 there was 34.7% residential and only 26.5% vacant land.

The residential area in turn was distributed in Hyderabad South 24.9%, North 63.3% and Secunderabad 11.8%, and the vacant land in Hyderabad South was 2.6%, North 51.8% and Secunderabad 45.6%. Vijaya Bhole (1985). Further the city by the year 1981 as per the census had 59.4% Hindus 37.6% Muslims, Telugu was spoken by 47.2% and Urdu by 37.5% of the city's population. During the year 1985 Vijaya found Hyderabad South had only 12% Hindus, North 56.5% and Secunderabad 32%. Whereas Muslim in Hyderabad South were to a tune of 70%, North 25% and only 5% were in the Secunderabad. Her analysis further showed Urdu was spoken in Hyderabad South by 75% people North 18% and Secunderabad 7%. And Telugu, in the South Hyderabad was spoken by 20% people North by 50% and Secunderabad by 30% of people. Barriers like language and religion played a vital role in the urban land-use. Localities with homogeneous cultures and communities emerged distinctly. This again reflected on the land use pattern of the city.

By the year 1981 Hyderabad city had 455 slums distributed in Hyderabad South 138, North 243 and in Secunderabad 72 reported by Municipal Corporation of Hyderabad. Vijaya (1985) found the level of satisfaction of neighbourhood and living conditions were best in Hyderabad North 28%, and it was unsatisfactory in South 35%. Distinctly, the migrants from the slums have changed their residences to better civic zones. Thereby, residential mobility and the city slum land use pattern also has undergone transformation.

Purchase of Plots by the Repatriates: Occupation-wise

The occupational category-wise and income-wise purchase of house plots after their migration in the cardinal direction-wise of the city (see Tables 5.22 and 5.23).

It is observed that in general the repatriates distributed all over the city had purchased plots for residence all over the city. Except North eastern side of the fringe areas (2.9%) the other cordial directions has above ten per cent localisation of plots. The North-east of the urban fringe of Hyderabad mainly constitutes of the newly emerging industrial residential townships. The repatriates mainly Muslims are not interested in this direction, for they don't have neither their culture prevalent nor adequate civic facilities and good environment to attract these people in this direction of the city. The land for residence is very cheap in this direction, as the area is polluted

Table 5.22

Location of Residential Plots - Cardinal direction-wise - Hyderabadi workers repatriated from Kuwait (Occupation-wise)

Occupation	*East*	*South East*	*South*	*South West*	*West*	*North West*	*North*	*North East*	*Total*
Professionals	5.9	5.9	5.9	23.5	23.5	17.6	17.6	-	100
Technicians	6.3	12.5	25.0	18.8	6.3	18.8	6.3	6.3	100
Service workers	11.8	23.5	5.9	17 6	-	23.5	11.8	5.9	100
Drivers	11.8	14.7	16.2	17.6	8.8	17.6	10.3	2.9	100

Source: Sample Survey - Hyderabad - 1991.

Table 5.23

Location of Residential Plots - Cardinal direction-wise - Hyderabadi workers repatriated from Kuwait (Income-wise)

Occupation	*East*	*South East*	*South*	*South West*	*West*	*North West*	*North*	*North East*	*Total*
Below 10,000	50.0	16.7	33.3	-	-	-	-	-	100
10,001-20,000	20.0	26.7	26.7	6.7	-	13.4	6.7	-	100
20,001-30,000	12.5	12.5	25.0	18.8	12.5	18.5	-	-	100
30,001-50,000	-	15.0	20.0	10.0	25.0	25.0	-	5.0	100
Above 50,000	9.1	9.1	27.3	9.1	18.2	18.2	9.1	-	100
Total	13.2	21.7	16.2	14.7	5.0	14.7	5.0	3.3	100

Source: Sample Survey -Hyderabad - 1991.

due to industries to a certain extent and is covered by various other research institutions and also physically is a rugged and rough terrain. Besides, this zone has never been a cultural hearty of the city. The bondage of culture, language and religion with the old city is weak. Hence, this zone does not show any impact of migration.

A large chunk of the repatriates (35.2%) constituting 17.6% each in the North west and South west of the city have purchased their residential plots. It appears that the North-east and South-east of the city make a semi-circle of mostly the Hindu community, migrants from all over the South of Andhra and industrial units. The semi-circle of North-west and South-west constitutes mainly Muslims and this also has industries but the local and native population of the Hyderabad city incorporate in this sector. This is mainly due to the age-old cultural affinity.

Rao (1990) has observed in his social ecology of Hyderabad that the North-west and North is the very high and rich ranked sector of the city and the North-east and East are marked as high ranking social area by his factorial ecology concept and calculation. The centre of the city has medium social rank and all the south, south west and south east are the low categorized zones.

The repatriates of lower cadre preferred to occupy the South (16.2%), South-west (17.6%). This goes again with the history repeats itself concept. The historic core and the historic origin of the city starated from the South-west where Golconda Fort is located. When the city of Hyderabad was built further south of Musi river all the people shifted to this area leaving the fort area in decay. Presently the new generation natives of the Hyderabad old are in the process of retrieving towards these remnant parts of the city. Once again the relicts and derelicts of Golconda in and around area is the most preferred of the repatriates in general and the muslim community in particular.

A large number of new colonies have emerged in the South-west of Hyderabad.The campus of Hyderabad Central University is located in this direction. The main highway connecting Charminar, Mehdipatnam, Toli Chowki, Dargah, Shaikpet area eventually connecting in semi-circular with the South-west, West and North-west of the city has become very rich. The vacant lands both Hillocks, plain lands all are marked of plots. Construction activity of posh localities, new houses, market areas, entertainment, and other land use is conspicuous in and around Golconda Fort.

Plotting, re-plotting, new roads, a large and frequent number of buses, good network of roads, interior the colonies and more organized structural development is featured and fathered in this semi-circle of the metropolis.

The table on income-wise purchase of residential, plots show that South-east and South of the urban periphery is dominated 21.7% and 16.2% respectively. The South-west and North-west 14.7% each is the next opted direction. The west of Hyderabad urban fringe is mainly constituted of Hyderabad Central University. This is a transition area between the North-west industrial fringe and the South-west predominant residential zone which is emerging as the rich city zone of the metropolis.

The process of purchase of plots initiated immediately when the repatriates started to think of a house of their own in the most secluded areas. Almost over a decade from 1970 to 1980 the purchase of plots was continued. The construction of houses (73.5%) maximum was undertaken by 1985-90. This was the period when the cost of land, material for construction have reached to peaks. A large number of repatriates engaged themselves as commission agents for supply of construction materials and also as Auto Consultants services which does not require any investment at all. Having plenty of free time and most of their financial assets in the Banks and the rich experience of purchasing plots, construction of their own houses created a confidence and carrier for these people, the lower cadre did the commission agent business and the professional repatriates undertook architectural design plans contractor business etc. Eventually an amalgam of these professionals created joint institutional efforts of building flats in the posh and attractive areas which were sold and booked by the prospective repatriates and the rich citizens of the society. With a little and intial investment and with the advances paid by the customers it became quite easy for these people to multiply their future ventures and it spread all over the city. Suburb's and peripheries of the metropolis.

Observation revealed that the outskirts of the city land is purchased in acres from the land-lords or "pattadars" (owners of land).

Plots are marked of different sizes, sold out on cash or instalment to the institutional workers for colonies or for the individual accommodation. This process and activity is observed all over fringe of the city. The repatriates purchased a number of plots on cash. Most of such plots are re-sold on high profits and the rest is kept for more profit speculations.

Inside the city, old buildings are purchased at appropriate commercial and residential localities and are pulled down. The same space is converted into a complex emerging with a number of residential blocks and commercial shops etc. All over the city it is found that this activity is in its full galore grand and gacity all over the metropolitan Hyderabad.

Hence, it is concluded, that the building activity and the emergence of new houses is clearly the result of the migration of the large number of youth from Hyderabad to Gulf. They realised that real estate is the only and the best form of investment and prosperity. The city of Hyderabad particularly the old city is loosing its traditional culture and character. Both residential and commercial activity is undergoing a drastic and tremendous transformation. The hub of the city has witnessed a lot of residential renovation and vertical development, besides, all the vacant lands are occupied and new colonies have emerged.

The urban fringe areas of the metropolis, particularly the south, south-east and south-west, which are basically the material quarters are significantly transformed. The physical growth of the city in these directions is attributed with the material mobility of the migrants and the repatriates. The northern periphery of the city is mainly industrial in nature.

The city of Hyderabad, at present is undergoing a mass using transformation, numerous multi-storey buildings with one, two or three bed-room are constructed and sold either an cash or installment. Loans are arranged for the working class by the agents and brokers.

Hence, it is concluded that the "culture of construction" is an outcome of the Gulf migration, it appears that the trend has taken off and shall be continued for over a decade. The city of Hyderabad is geographically the most suitable for physical growth. Hence, horizontal expansion is inevitable clubbed with virtual Development of Housing.

REFERENCES

Ball M. and Kirwan M. (1976), "Accessibility and supply constraints in the urban housing markets", Urban Studies, Vol. 14.

Basset K. and Short J. (1980), "Housing and Residential structure and alternative approaches", London.

Bhole Vijaya (1980), "Housing and urban development in India", Classical Publishing Co., New Delhi.

Bourne L. and Hitchcock J. (1979), "Urban housing markets", "Recent Directions in Research and Policy", University of Toronto Press.

Eisen Stadt S.N. (1953), "Analysis of patterns of immigration and absorption of immigrants", Population studies, 7.

Hagarstand T. (1957), "Migration and Area - Survey of a sample of Swedish migration fields and hypothetical considerations of their genesis".

Julian Wolpert (1970), "Behavioural aspects of decision to migrate", in population geography A reader - By G.J. Deko, McGraw Hill.

Mangalam J.J. (1968), "Human migration", University of Kentuchy Press, Lexington, K.Y.

Ratna Naidu (1987), "Old cities and new predicaments".

Thomos D.S. (1954), "Population re-distribution and economic growth", U.S. - American Philosophical Society.

Turner J. (1976), "Housing by people", Marion Boyars, London.

Weinberg A.A. (1961), "Migration and belonging : A study of mental health and personal adjustment in Israel".

Zelinshy (1971), "The hypothesis of mobility Transitions", Geographical Review, 61.

6
SUMMARY AND CONCLUSIONS

For over past two decades, the Indian Muslims have been temporarily migrating to the South West Asian Countries in search of employment. The petroleum boom in these countries has attracted labour from all over the Asian countries. They constituted the skilled, semi-skilled and un-skilled labour force in South West Asian countries. Basically, this exodus was the outcome of heavy unemployment and resultant frustration which led to this phenomenon to a considerable extent. Other than the unemployed youth, most of the settled employees also could not withstand the lure of this attractive economic opportunity. They either applied for leave, lien or simply fled their professions to hunt for the overwhelming treasure to gear up their social and economic perspectives.

In India heavy response was noted from the state of Kerala, followed by Hyderabad in Andhra Pradesh. Majority of the minority population from these states made their fortunes earnestly waiting for them. At the beginning of this process, only skilled personnel were appointed and were paid attractively. In the latter stages it was the semi-skilled and the unskilled workers who followed. Although the lure was not a dream, lest it started like a nightmare but ended in reality. Score of individuals, sometimes groups who were allured to this attraction have also failed, disappointed and left for nowhere. Sufferings were awaiting them after their return and failure of success in the host country. They had to accept the realities of life. Such people definitely were hit by acute economic crisis; their assets were lost, heavy debts engulfed and surrounded them. Courage and physical fitness paved ways for such misfortunates. Nevertheless, a few of them were able to recover the shock earnestly; others are still reeling under the shadow of socio-economic darkness and disappointment. Yet another group of households are awaiting to play this gamble, the thirst of these people in increasing. To quench this, they are taking various risks to admonitor their dream and the dreams of their household members. They feel whatsoever is the result would certainly be better than to struggle in their existing economic cradle. They are constantly trying and re-trying to reach their destiny. Such house-holds are in a stress and strain of debts and false promises awaiting to see the brighter side of their forthcoming future.

Realising the variety of outcome, sometimes with a treasure and sometimes disappointed in this process of movement, Government of India in all its efforts has established various betterment schemes to invest their assets into banks, industries, commerce etc. It has also opened cells for looking and to investigate into the disappointed and is attempting by all means to rehabilitate such personnel with certain programmes and policies.

Despite their concern, many governments of the developing countries failed to provide basic information needed to better understand this temporary migratory movement and to develop sound policy responses. Social, economic and political institutions of the developing countries generated motivation for migration and the momentum for the differential population growth of regions and of nations as a whole.

Over the past decade, actual experience and scientific case studies revealed the great variety of long term and temporary migratory movements. It is deemed advisable to focus on a distinct aspects of this temporary movements, approached at the most appropriate levels of analysis (the individual, the households the communities) and at different levels of geographic aggregation (the city, the region, the nation and the international sub-system).

The wider process of unequal regional and sectorial development which altered the division of labour and the occupational mix, created an international labour market. Temporary migrants were often very important for firms of the larger cities and resources potential regions depended on short-term contracts, high labour turnover and low wages and other operating costs. In all these operations, migration, urbanisation and employment were constantly getting reviewed in the third world countries.

During the mid 1970's the steep increase in the oil prices created an economic boost in the south west asian countries, particularly Saudi Arabia, Kuwait, Bahrain, UAE. Obviously this phenomenon initiated to a process of industrialisation of these countries. In order to stimulate and exonerate industrialisation needed the employment. The employment of cheap and skilled labour which was lying in drains in the Asian countries was captured by the developed nations. USA, France, Korea, Japan etc., who have leased big contracts to mobilise industrialisation in the Gulf countries. These countries hired labour of all types on contract basis to work in their various projects, construction works etc.

This phenomenon in the third world countries left a deep economic impression. The call for labour was well attended and respond mainly from Pakistan, Indonesia, India, Bangladesh, Philippines, Korea and other countries. This cosmopolitan mixture of races, skills mobilized the process of oil exploration, exploitation of resources, industrialization and urbanisation in all over south-west Asia. The impact was felt in a fewer pockets of the neighbouring countries which were basically under developed economically suppressed, but have not raised substantially in their standards of living.

As was already mentioned that in India most of the minority youth particularly from Kerala dominantly participated in the exodus followed by the Hyderabadis. The later were living in acute unemployment, low literacy, third rate standards of living, dilapidated housing conditions, social stress, economic strain, heavy domestic burden, historical and political isolation was the call of the day for these frustrated younger generation of the muslim community in the historic core city of Hyderabad which compelled these youths to throng at once to this economic fortune call.

Obviously, the receipt of remittances drastically relived their economic pain and improved their socio-economic profile of the community in particular and the city of Hyderabad in general. Improved facade of house, renovated internally and externally to a typical Islamic style, adoring of Arab dressing, Arabic language, costly perfume bearing and a typical Arabian style was adopted amongst the muslims of the old Hyderabad house-holds. The change was not only reflected internally but was also exhibited externally in almost all walks of life styles. It went a long way in alluring their children, relatives, neighbours and all other kith and kins closer and farther.

Majority of these fortunate ones were constantly helping the unfortunate ones to join the stream. They started to give heavy charities, donations generously for the development and construction of mosques etc. The whole morphology of the old Hyderabad has changed. Be it a banana vendor, vegetable vendor, a hotel bearer, a pan shop owner a cycle repairer, a taxi driver, a bootlegger, a vagabond or a clerk, a doctor, an engineer exploited this opportunity to their fullest capacities.

As a result of this economic boom, commendable changes, transformations came into the life of an individual, the household, the community and finally it also resulted to a considerable extent in the morphological outlook, spatial growth and the urban development of the city of Hyderabad. The people who are starved, poverty stricken became rich within a short span of time. This resulted into mis-management of the remittances. Illiteracy, improper understanding and utilisation of the money reflected into a normal means of daily life. The groceries, the land values, the rentals, the amenities all shot up due to substantial money power of these persons in the city.

The city of Hyderabad experienced a big change in the consumer behaviour, vertical and horizontal growth and development of housing became evident everywhere. High traffic congestion, numerous motor cycles, varieties of commercial activities picked up in all the commercial centres of the city. The number of schools got multiplied, professional education, coupled with centres of smaller skills, para-medical training and allied institutions emerged to impart the skills in demand in the Gulf.

The Asian Regional Team for Employment Promotion (ARTEP). A ILO study, on the impact of return migration found that, their reabsorption into gainful employment may be hindered by certain adverse consequences of migration on the economy. One of them is that the wages have increased, not productivity, leading to inflation, second is the growing use of the capital intensive technology due to skilled production workers. Thirdly the adverse impact of migration on skills development in the informal sector.

The limited use of remittances on productive ventures, higher expenditure on construction and tertiary sector, particularly, hotel business, cinemas, may not flourish long.

ARTEP recommended on the issue of return migrants, that stronger measures to channel remittances into productive investments, to influence technology choices in favour of labour intensive instead of capital intensive activities, and to expand the possibilities for acquiring needed skills at low cost.

On the welfare measures, a majority of the returnees to benefit schemes like investments in school and health activities in the towns and cities, low cost life insurance policies (popular in Pakistan) encouragement on small savings, creating institutions responsible for implementation of various government programmes for NRIs. Finally, legislature powers to the government to intervene in the labour migration process. Also co-operation between government and private sector are recommended.

The exodus of the muslim community for a temporary durations in the middle eastern countries for better economic opportunities in the city of Hyderabad has brought a tremendous change. The socio-economic conditions of this community has drastically changed. The way of thinking has also changed. The economic stability provided a far reaching impact on the housing and culture. The workers who have sacrificed their regular employment, which they with difficulty have acquired left and join the stream of migrants towards the Gulf. It is observed that their decision was fruitful and meaningful. They have realised that even if would have completed their superannuation in India and be provided with pension could not have made them happy. The Gulf employment provided a lots of satisfaction in terms of work, boarding and lodging, health facilities, schooling for children.

The lucrature pay and perks has considerably changed the lives of the people. In many instances they have helped their closer kith and kin. They had generously participated on the religions activities, by regularly paying "Zakat". They had also contributed large amounts for the renovation and construction of mosques all over the city of Hyderabad. They undertook the task of celebrating their childrens and sisters marriages with gaity and splendour. The older parents were well looked after. They have also liked to stay in joint families, this had made their stay abroad easy. During their absence, their children were mixed with the other members of the joint family.

The migrants to the Gulf in general were behind the Real Estates and Vacant plots and lands. In addition to the Gold and other valuable assets at home, they preferred to own a plot to build a house of their own choice and locality. This become true for many of the migrants.

The city outskirts particularly, the South West and Western side which was vacant was grabbed by the migrants. The idea was cheap and more land. They intended to build a double storey since it would also give them sufficient rent. However, the idea of leaving houses tolet was only limited to those who were unskiiled and or were drawing low salaries. The migrants at the higher echelons with good salaries never waited their house to be let on rent : This is because they felt the problems of rentors, secondly they felt the need of a separate independent house stay during the two months leave period which they avail once in two years. Hence, they preferred to accommodate their own people, free of rent and whenever they come, they expected them to keep vacant their house.

A number of the migrants have also were in possession of a telephone and car. The usage of telephone was so acute that they can speak to home whenever they want from abroad. It was like staying at home. Hence, they were paying anything to obtain a telephone for easy communications. The car was necessary for the whole family to move easily whenever they wanted to do so.

The children choice and likes and dislikes were usually upheld. Better schooling was always searched. They realised the value of education, which for most of the migrants was a scarcity during their childhood. Hence, they undertook extraordinary care towards the educational needs of their children.

The main drawback of the migrants was the unproductive utilisation of financial resources. The bulk amount received every month gave them a freedom to spend lavishly without even bargain. They started to eye on quality than quantity. They were the indirect contributions for the excess rates on the essential goods, land, housing and so on. The native citizens could not compete with the migrants. The so-called "Nawabs" of the Hyderabad also were not in a position to compete their standards of living, purchasing power and bank balance. Hence, the economic conditions tilted. The concept of poverty has changed. At the beginning with large families, most of the families have experienced a bitter poverty and life style.

The two and half decade of Gulf exodus has brought a terrible infrastructural change in the physical and cultural outlook of the city. The commercial culture of the city also has undergone a drastic change numerous new bazars in the old city of Hyderabad cropped up. It is observed that those members of the migrant family who could not or never waited to go abroad have taken up business on a large scale with the financial assistance of the migrant member at Hyderabad. They have learnt a lot in the constructions and transportation sections. Their expertise was also in the cloth and shoe business. Hence, it is found that a majority of such incumbents created a new business culture in the city or Hyderabad. They have started to purchase the foreign cloth and electronic goods from the middle east and a few pockets of the old city streets were confined for such foreign material. In addition to this they also were selling the country made goods. Once the market was established, it became a regular feature for their future. In this endeavour the relatives and others staying in Middle East themselves started helping them by sending or getting along with them a number of watches, cloth and other costly material which has a ready sale in the Hyderabad Market.

The physical outlook of the city has also tremendously changed. The roads were widened, the drainage and other civic amenities were made abundant. There was one or two taps in every house for drinking water. The public taps in the old city of Hyderabad, particularly in certain posh localities have disappeared. The increase in the vehicular traffic keeps the city roads busy all over the day. A large number of tea and pan shops have emerged all over the city.

The interior vacant lands, the vacant palaces, the smaller hillocks, ponds and green patches were filled up of residential occupants. Most of such lands are encroached with the connivance of the administrative officials. The people had to only get "Notary" and start build a house. They are given a municipal number, provided with a tap, drainage, and electricity. They regularly pay the house and land tax to the revenue department. Hence all such residents are closely associated in their problems to fight the government by legal means whenever there is trouble.

The plight of the repatriated community from Kuwait to Hyderabad is otherwise. These people were "Lords" before their return. They had a substantial period of stay in Kuwait. However, the unfortunate accession of Kuwait by Iraq came as a death blow. No one had imagined such a human disaster. Almost all the Hyderabadis staying in Kuwait had returned. Secondly, when they were in Hyderabad, before they could get out of the shock, they encountered another by way of communal tension and curfew in the city of Hyderabad. This again came as a shock of these repatriates. They mentally agreed that they should never go elsewhere and look after their families in Hyderabad.

A large number of the repatriates had come with nothing with them. Some were escorted by the government. Other fled of their own through the land route by car from Kuwait to Hyderabad. This was indeed a life time experience for such people.

The remittances already sent by the repatriates of the Kuwait were spent without any productive use. No one speculated the disaster. There was a mental turmoil and agony for such people. They have started to re-assemble their skills and other resources left over by them before their migration. Many of the professionals and others who were employed before migration started to resume back to their old employment. The technicians have picked up their neglected skills and started living a fresh. The service oriented people were worst hit. They had no better opportunities in Hyderabad as they enjoyed in Kuwait. It came very difficult for them to rehabilate and procure a job for themselves. Besides the age-bar also became a liability in such cases. The category of Drivers at once started to earn after their return. In most of the cases they had owned a transport vehicle or on auto rickshaw, they started working in the same old fashion and were the least bothered ones. However, most of the potential drivers were recalled by the Kuwaiti Government after its being freed from Iraq.

On the 2nd of August, 1990 Iraq had suddenly seized Kuwait, this unwarranted move was criticized by the whole world. The peaceful and prosperous state like Kuwait was always rendering economic support by importing labour from all the underdeveloped countries of Asia and the Arabs in particular, with the Iraqi invasion the whole economy was shattered. The Royal family the Ruler, and all the immigrant workers fled the country. The devastation was total, the control nerve of the Kuwait, its oil industry had been completely burnt. From the economic point of view, no less than from Environment perspective, the greatest damage was that inflicted on the oil industry. The destruction of refineries and pipelines and storage systems and above all. The firing of more than 600 oil wells was brought unprecedented catastrophe to the economy and the environment of Kuwait.

During the mid-1990, Kuwait had a population of 2.1 million. There were 800,000 Kuwaiti citizens and above 50 per cent of them were below 25 years of age. 90 per cent of the total population was in urban areas and mostly located along the coast. The life expectancy for men and women was 71 and 75 years respectively. The infant mortality rate was 15 per 1000. Education, health were virtually free to both the Kuwaitis and the immigrants, housing was subsidized for low and middle income groups. The per capita income amounted to about $US 14,700 and the GDP in 1989 was $ 11,600.

In brief, Kuwait in mid 1990, had a solid balance of payment position, public finances were under control and the process of industrialisation and improved development of human resources was proceeding apace, economic instability was still somewhat inherent in the development process of the country because of the volatility of oil prices and unusually high reliance on migrant labour. However, Kuwait had a functioning economy and was clearly poised to attain even higher living standards and still greater social development in the years ahead.

The invasion of Kuwait by Iraq brought about a dramatic change. By the end of Iraq's occupation on 26 February 1991, the outlook has been radically transformed. Kuwait city, previously a modern urban centre with thriving bazaars and a busy commercial district, had become a ghost town. The some was true of the other urban areas of the country. Two-thirds of the Kuwait nationals had sought refuge abroad, three-quarters of the immigrant labour force left Kuwait. Health, Education and other essential services had come to a complete halt.

The impact of economic and commercial life of Kuwait was also devastating. The physical infrastructure supporting basic services - electricity, water, waste disposal - had been rendered inoperative. Ports largely destroyed, oil production and refining crippled, financial system disrupted. foreign trade suspended, commerce considerably diminished, manufacturing paralyzed, and inventories plundered.

The marine environment of Kuwait had been severely affected by the flow of crude oil in the Persian Gulf, while the beautiful water front in Kuwait city had been devastated and its entire beach turned into a mine field. The process of rehabilitation is in its initial stage. The physical infrastructure could well require a great part of the present decade to recover. The harm to the population from a polluted environment although not easily identifiable today, may become manifest in a pervasive way only with the passage of time. Plans for the restoration of social and administrative services are being formulated on an urgent basis. But it will take months, even years before the country recovers, and attain a self reliant, clean and healthy atmosphere.

The international relations linked with the gulf crisis to evaculate the migrants. Approximately 350,000 people were repatriated by their own governments under bilateral or tripartite arrangements. The Indian Government took a leading role in repatriating not only its citizens, but also others from the South Asian countries. Jordan became a focal transit point of over 750,000 - era areas from other countries, who were assisted by various international agencies. Nearly 156,000 migrants were airlifted from Jordan, Turkey, Iraq & Iran under the auspices of the Geneva based United Nations International Organisation for Migration.

A United Nations compensation commission was established and the ILO has assisted in assessing the financial loss, the claims and others. The UN Development programme, the IMF and the World Bank cooperated to provide emergency financial assistance. An estimated 2 million claimants were expected to lodge claims. Asians were the majority who were effected due to the Gulf War. Some of the Asians instead of returning back to their countries preferred to reach Hong Kong, Singapore and Japan.

Addressing the UN compensation commission, the UN Secretary General Boutros Ghali called for funds by 1994 end to compensate victims of Iraq's 1990-91 invasion and occupation of Kuwait. His appeal was directed at the 40 countries that have Frozen Iraqi Oil assets and are resisting handing part of them over to the United Nations. The Commission set up by the UN Security Council, has received $ 125 billion worth claims from civilians., corporations and governments. However, only United States handed over $ 200 million to UN of the Iraqi Oil assets. The rest have refused and are holding the assets against their own national claims.

The United Nations compensation commission has provided "Forms" for the following claims viz.:

1. Damages, arising from departure from Iraq or Kuwait, Inability to leave Iraq or Kuwait, a decision not to return to Iraq or Kuwait, hostage taking or other Illegal Detention;
2. Damages arising from personal injury;
3. Damages arising from the death of spouse, child or parent;
4. Personal property losses;
5. Loss of Bank Accounts, Stocks and other Securities;
6. Loss of income, unpaid salaries or support;
7. Real property losses;
8. Individual business losses.

At Hyderabad, the Kuwaiti repatriates have formed into a Association IKF. At a nominal rate of Rs. 50/- individuals are registered. At the beginning the association has requested the Government of Andhra Pradesh to immediately provide them with Gas cylinders and Ration cards. They have also requested that their children be admitted into all the schools irrespective of the Academic year being commenced. The other details related to Indo-Kuwait Friendship (IKF) have been collected from the members of the association by visiting their office personally.

The Association in several occasions met the Kuwaiti ambassador at New Delhi. They had also represented their problems to the union ministers, chief minister and minister for Minority Affairs. They have decided to hold an exhibition and a symposium on India-Kuwait Friendship from 23 to 27 February 1994. They have invited the union ministers alongwith the Kuwait Ambassador to India. This opportunity is intended to appraise the ministers and the officials to look into their genuine problems and assist them in either being rehabilitated in India or send them to Kuwait in their original positions.

The Association has registered about 1700 applicants. They claimed that all over Andhra Pradesh about 8000 Kuwaiti repatriates are spread all over the districts. The city of Hyderabad alone is expected to have about 5000 repatriates.

As per their understanding the workers who have returned to Kuwait are very few. They felt most of the fewer workers have left to Kuwait from all over India and other countries. The Association General Secretary has felt that 60 per cent of the Drivers category, 20% of the professionals, mostly Engineers, Technicians 10 per cent and 5 per cent of the service people have returned back to Kuwait from those who were repatriated. Others are all waiting for their claims from United Nations. Most of the workers from the Health Ministry have returned from Hyderabad. Maid servants almost everyone has left.

A private agency has initiated to help the repatriates get back their claim from the Government, Kafeel, the UN Security Council in Geneva on a commission basis of 7 per cent. The Ministry of External Affairs of the Central Government has opened a special cell for the Kuwaitis. They are providing forms of claims from the UN and forwarding the same to Geneva for further scrutiny and compensation payment. The workers who had their "stay or residence permit or "Aqama" beyond August 1990, on production of such a witness of work permit and others are paid their full salaries till the date of expiry of the residence permit. Other perks are however not paid. Hence, workers, who would have stayed beyond 1990 have produced the evidence and have already received their salaries. Presently, the Minister for Minority Affairs of Andhra Pradesh has promised to recommend the Banks to release loans for self employment and other business ventures. The Association is optimistic of receiving of such an assistance.

The first hypothesis of the study was to study the drastic socio-economic transformation of the Kuwaiti repatriates since 1970s, which proved in their better way of living, housing, purchase power and so on. This was proved true from the survey analysis. However, this was only when the workers were in Kuwait. But after return their condition is dilapidating.

The second hypothesis was the wasteful expenditure of their remittances in home town. This was also proved positive presently, the repatriates are pained at their unmindful ways and waste of money. As long as they were in Kuwait their family members, spouse and others have relentlesly spent the remittances. This often was concerned by the workers. However, they never speculated that they have to undergo the trauma of invasion and consequently return to home town to find nothing much is left of their past remittances.

Thirdly, the occupational shift of the workers from Hyderabad to Kuwaiti and back to Hyderabad has resulted in negative. The skills and work learnt at Kuwait does not suit the working conditions of their home town. They are relactant to accept their old jobs, hence are facing difficulties to find new works.

Fourthy, the morphological structure, urbanisation and commercial culture of the city of Hyderabad particularly, the old city has undergone a tremendous transformation. Besides, the urban fringe has witnessed a large new residential buildings and planned colonies resulting in the physical expansion of the city. This development is the contribution of all the migrants of Hyderabad to various South-West Asian countries. However, the Kuwaiti repatricates also form part of their contribution.

Fifthly, the urban fringe also witnessed purchase of plots and kept vacant only to resale on higher rates. This speculation proved true. Most of the repatriates either storted constructing a new house or are selling on higher rates due to heavy demand.

Lastly, the migration trend of the Hyderabadis to various south-west Asian countries including Kuwait elevated the purchase and living standards high. Obviously, the local non-migrated citizens strongly felt the competation. This was also proved positive.

Suggestions

Based on the preceding study the following suggestions, are made to ameliorate the problems of the Kuwaiti repatriated workers to Hyderabad:

1. The Indian Government, need to take positive stand on the Indo-Kuwait relationship. Though the Ministry of External Affairs, Government of India has opened a special cell to monitor the compensation benefits to the workers. This measure itself may not lead to any concrete results. Ample scope

exists to take up other issues of expatriation and collaboration in various other fields of technological know how and other bilateral relations between the two countries.

2. Indias Foreign Policy of the south-west Arab nations needs to be well defined and there should a long-term plan. The Indo-Pakistan problem often obscures to promote diplomatic ties between these countries and India. However, Kuwait is in the process of emerging back to its original position after the devastation of Iraqi invasion. The Indians have already served Kuwait and are yet willing to do so, obviously, it is ripe time to initiate negotiations and take a positive stand of sincerely coordinating in the re-development process of Kuwait. Such as action would go a long way in maintaining better relations in future.
3. India should formulate a policy with regard to the problems of return migration of workers, businessmen and others. Today it is Kuwait, next it could be any other country from where Indians would repatriate. Hence, permanent and comprehensive plan of rehabilitation should be drawn in advance by the government. The Non-Resident Indians financial contributions have always helped the government in various ways. In turn the government policy both in promoting their rehabilitation and expatriation need to be a prime concern in boosting the economic base on the one hand and solving the unemployment problem on the other of our country.
4. The Government of Andhra Pradesh being well equipped with a large number of research consultants, planners and developmental institutions based at Hyderabad such as ANRICH (Andhra Pradesh State Non-Resident Indians Investment Corporation Ltd.), APITCO (Andhra Pradesh Industrial & Technological Consultancy Ltd.), IGB (Investment Guidance Bureau), and many others. It should try to pool all these to formulate plan schemes for the return migrants. A comprehensive survey and study shall be very useful in ameliorating their problems and possible developmental issues.

5. Restoration of their former jobs to the Kuwaiti repatriates, shall go a long way in helping the returned migrants rehabilitation by the government.

6. The Indo-Kuwaiti Friendship (IKF) association should classify their registered personnel bearing different skills and possible investment capacities. This can in turn be provided to the various self employment promoting agencies, both private and public, for further scrutiny and assistance for rehabilitation.

7. Co-operative societies can be registered of the repatriated members, so that their living conditions, housing, and other activities can be managed under a society by themselves.

8. The Banks can play a specific role by studying repatriates skills, potentials and investment capacity and provide them with appropriate financial and technical know-how.

9. Finally, the repatriates should very sensibly and productively invest their compensation money and join the main national stream. They can study the new economic policy of India and other packages of benefits and help themselves, rather than depending on any agency for their own rehabilitation.

10. The repatriated professionals and the technicians can combine their efforts to start a uni-industry on partnership basis and also request the government to allot free plots for such industries. The drivers obviously can try their luck in the transportation sector.

11. It is strongly felt that the amount which is expected to be received in the form of compensation from the United Nations would be grossly misused. Instead, the government can provide them with pension for a stipulated period and the same amount can be used by the government. This would be a better help than simply handing over the money. As these incumbents have already has substantial loans raised, a larage amount would be paid back from their compensation claim. The remaining would be spent for domestic consumption. It

is observed that these people have already joined the stream of normal natives. They have realised that going back to Kuwait may not be an happy occasion due to the devastation. However, with the money received through compensation may be utilised to go to other middle eastern countries by purchasing a working visa. The present problem of these repatriated workers is going to drastically change with the receipt of compensation. However, there is a scope to take up a study on the utilisation and consumption pattern of the money to be received by March/April 1994.

BIBLIOGRAPHY

Abu Lughod, J. (1961) 'Migrant adjustment to city life; the Egyptian case', *American Journal of Sociology*, 67, 22-72.

Adams, J.S. (1969) 'Directional bias in intro-urban migration, *Economic Geography*, 45, 302-23.

Adams, R.B. (1969) 'United States Metropolitan migration: Dimension and predictability, *Proceedings of the Association of American Geographers*, 1, 1-6.

Aldkogius, M. (1970) 'Population change and urban growth', *Geografiska Annaler*, 52B, 131-40.

Allon-Smith, R.D. (1978) 'The Migration of the Elderly: a Social Geography,' unpublished Ph.D. Thesis, University of Leicester.

Alperovich, G., Bergsman, J. and Eheman, C. (1977) 'An econometric model of migration between United States metropolitan areas', *Urban Studies*, 14, 135-45.

Alvarez, J.H. (1967) *Return Migration to Puerto Rico*, University of California Press, Berkeley.

Ambrose, P. and Colenutt, R. (1975) *The Property Machine*, Penguin, Harmondsworth.

Amin, S. (ed.) (1974) *Modern Migration in Western Africa*, Oxford University Press, London.

Bassett, K. and Short, J.R. (1978) 'Housing improvements in the inner city, a case study of changes before and after 1974 Housing Act', *Urban Studies*, 15, 333-42.

Abdo Mohammad Fowzi (1988), *The Urbanisation of Kuwait since 1950: Planning Progress and Issues,* Ph.D. Thesis.

Ahmad Mansoor (1982), "Emigration of Scare skills in Pakistan ILO, International Migration for employment", *Working Paper No.* 5, Geneva.

Akbar Mahmood (1981), "Pakistan: Emigration for employment", Report of ARPLA, Symposium on overseas recruitment, ILO, Islamabad, May 1981.

Al-Dafiri, Abdul Wahad Mohammad (1987), "Women, Labour Force participation, and Equality: A study of educated women in Kuwait", Ph.D. Thesis.

Al-Ghabra Shafeeq Nazem (1987), "Palestinians in Kuwait: The family and politics of survival", Ph.D. Thesis.

Al-Ghazali, Essa Mohammed (1989), "Human Resource Policies and the welfare state administration in Kuwait", Ph.D. Thesis.

Al-Moosa-Abdul Rasool (1988), "Salaried employment — A consequences of urbanisation in Kuwait", *Journal of Social Sciences,* 16, 121-141.

Al-Moosa-Kerith Mclahn (1985), "Immigrant Labour in Kuwait".

Al-Najadah, Abdulla Fozan Al Fozan (1989), "Social change and Alienation in Kuwait", Ph.D. Thesis.

Al-Ofariba, Obaid Srour (1988), "Shopping Centre Development and Consumer Behaviour in Kuwait", Ph.D. Thesis.

Al-Sahhaf Habbeb (1990), "Human Resource Management in Kuwait", Ph.D. Thesis.

Al-Shayeji, Abdullah Khalifah (1988), "Democratization in Kuwait: The National Assembly as a strategy for political survival", Ph.D. Thesis.

Ali Syed Ashraf et al. (1981), "Labour migration from Bangla Desh to Middle East", *World Bank•Staff Working Paper No. 454,* Washington, D.C.

Allah Mohammad (1989), "The composition and growth of the labour force in Kuwait", Ph.D. Thesis

Beals, R.E., Levy, M.A. and Moses, L. (1967) "Rationality and migration in Ghana", *Review of Economic Statistics*, 49, 480-6.

Beaujeau-Garnier, J. (1966) *Geography of Population*, Longman, London.

Bell, C. (1977) "On housing classes", *Australian and New Zealand Journal of Sociology*, 13, 36-40.

Bell, D.N.F. and Kirwan, F.X. (1979) "Return migration in a Scottish context", *Regional Studies*, 13, 36-111.

Berg, E. (1965) 'The economics of the Migrant labour system', in Kuper, H. (ed.), *Urbanization and Migration in West Africa*, University of California Press, Los Angeles.

Beshers, J.M. and Nishuira, E.N. (1961) 'A theory of internal migration differentials', *Social Forces*, 39, 214-18.

Board, C. (1976) The spatial structure of labour migration, Department of Geography, *Occasional Paper* No. 6, Queen Mary College.

Bogue, D.J. (1959) 'Internal migration'; in Hauser P.M. and Duncan, O.D. (eds.), *The Study of Population: An Inventory and Appraisal*, University of Chicago Press, Chicago, 486-509.

Bohning, W.R. (1972) *The Migration of Workers in the United Kingdom and the European Community*, Oxford University Press, London.

Bourne, L.S. (1976) 'Housing supply and housing market behaviour in residential development', in Herbert, D.T. and Johnston, R.J. (eds.), 111-58.

Brandes, S.H. (1975) *Migration, Kinship and Community*, Academic Press, New York.

Bright, M.L. and Thomas, D.S. (1941) 'Interstate migration and intervening opportunities', *American Sociological Review*, 6, 773-83.

Broek, J.O.M. and Webb, J.M. (1968) *The Geography of Mankind*, McGraw Hill, New York.

Brown, A.A. and Neuberger, E. (eds.) (1977) *Internal Migration: A Comparative Perspective*, Academic Press, New York.

Brown, J.S., Schwarzweller, H.K. and Mangalam, J.J. (1963) 'Kentucky Mountain migration and the Stem family: an American variation on the theme of Le Play', *Rural Sociology*, 28, 53-4.

Brown, L.A. (1970) 'On the use of Markov Chains in Movement Research', *Economic Geography*, 46, 393-403.

Brummell, A.C. (1979) 'A model of intra-urban mobility', *Economic Geography*, 55, 338-52.

Ball, M. and Kirwan, M. (1976), "Accessibility and supply constraints in the urban housing markets", *Urban Studies*, Vol. 14.

Basset, K. and Short, J. (1980), "Housing and Residential structure and alternative approaches", London.

Beaujean Gornier, J. (1966), "Geography of Population", Longman, London, p. 171.

Bhole Vijaya (1980), "Housing and urban development in India", Classical Publishing Co., New Delhi.

Birks, J.S. and Sinclair, C.A. (1980), *Arab Man Power: The Crisis of Development*, St. Martina Press, New York.

Bohning, W.R. (1984), "International migration: Implications for development policies", in UN, Department of International Economic and Social Affairs, Population Distribution, Migration and Development, pp. 379-403.

Boque, D.J. (1969). *op cit.*

Boque, J.J. (1969), *Principles of Demography*, Willey, New York, p. 752.

Bourne, L. and Hitchcock, J. (1979), "Urban housing markets: Recent Directions in Research and Policy", University of Toronto Press.

Brandes, S.H. (1975), *Migration, Leinship and Community*, Academic Press, New York.

Bu-Rasheed Add, J. (1988), "Crime among immigrants: A sociological study of crime in Kuwait", Ph.D. Thesis.

Cebula, R.J. (1980) *The Determinants of Human Migration*, Lexington Books, Lexington, Mass.

Cerase, F.P. (1974) 'Migration and social change : expectations and reality, A case study of return migration from the United States to Southern Italy', *International Migration Review*, 8, 245-62.

Clarke, J.I. (1965) Population Geography, Pergamon, Oxford.

Coollins, L. (1976) Introduction to Markov Chain Analysis, CATMOG No. 1, Geo Abstracts, Norwich.

Crompton, P.A. (1969) 'Internal migration and population change in Hungary between 1959 and 1965', Transactions, Institute of British Geographers, 47, 111-30.

Connell, J., Dasgupta, B., Laishley, R. and Lipton, M. (1976) Migration from Rural Areas, Oxford University Press, Delhi.

Conway, D. (1980) 'Stepwise migration: toward a classification of the mechanism', *International Migration Review*, 49, 3-14.

Crawford, C. (1966) 'Family attachment, family support for migration and migration plans of young people', *Rural Sociology*, 31, 293-310.

Chakravarthi, N.R. (1971), *The Indian Minorities in Burma: The Rise and Decline of the Immigrants Community*, Oxford University Press, London.

Clark and Moore (1980), "Residential Mobility and Public Policy", Urban Affairs - *Annual Review*, p. 19, New York.

Cleanson and Eqaro (1972), "Migration in Tanzania" - A review based in the 1967 population census - Research notes No. 1", University of Dar-es-Salam.

Deaton, B.J. and Anschel, K.R. (1974) "Migration and return migration: a new look at the eastern Kentucky migration streams", *Southern Journal of Agricultural Economics*, 6, 185-91.

Demko, D. (1974) 'Cognition of southern Ontario cities in a potential migration context', *Economic Geography*, 50, 20-34.

Duncan, S.S. (1976a) 'Research directions in social geography: housing opportunities and constraints', Transactions, Institute of *British Geographers*, N.S.I., 10-19.

Demery (1983), "Asian labour migration to the middle east", Paper presented in the conference - Asian labour migration to middle east - East-West centre, Honolulu, Sept. 1983.

Eisenstadt, S.N. (1953) 'Analysis of patterns of immigration and absorption of immigrants', *Population Studies*, 7, 167-80.

Edita, Tan (1983), "Adjustment of the labour market to the Foreign outflow of skilled labour - The case of construction workers", Bangkok, ARPLA, 1983.

Eisenstdet, S.N. (1953), "Analysis of patterns of immigration and absorption of immigrants", *Population Studies*, 7, pp. 167-180.

Ermisch, J. (1983), "The political economy of demographic change causes and implications of population trends in Great Britain", Heineman, London.

Farah Tawfic, E. (1989), "Population culture and Development in a Rentier State: The case of Kuwait", *Journal of African and Asian Studies*, 24, 1-2 Jan-April, pp. 106-113.

Farooq, G.M. (1975) "Population distribution and migration", in Robinson, W.C. (ed.), *Population and Development Planning*, Population Council, London, 134-52.

Farr, W. (1876), "Birth places of the people and the laws of migration", *Geographical Magazine*, 3, 35-37.

Ford, J. (1975) "The role of building society manager in the urban stratification system: autonomy *versus* constraint', *Urban Studies*, 12, 295-302.

Friedlander, D. (1970), "The spread of urbanization in England and Wales, 1851-1951", *Population Studies*, 24, 423-43.

Gale, S. (1973), "Explanation theory and models of migration", *Economic Geography*, 49, 257-74.

Galle, O.R. and Taeuber, K.E. (1966), "Metropolitan migration and intervening opportunities", *American Sociological Reviews*, 31, 5-13.

Gans, H. (1972) *People and Class,* Penguin, Harmondsworth.

Gaude, J. and Peek, P. (1970), "The economic effects of rural-urban migration", *International Labour Review,* 114, 329-38.

Gibbs, J.P. (1963), "The evolution of population concentrations", *Economic Geography,* 39, 340-50.

Girard, A., Bastide, H. and Pourcher, G. (1970), "Geographical mobility and urban concentration in France: a study in the provinces", in Jansen, A.J. (ed.), 203-55.

Gober-Meyers, P. (1978a), "Employment-motivated migration and economic growth in post-industrial market economies", Progress in Human Geography, 2, 207-29.

Gold, J.R. (1980), "An Introduction to Behavioural Geography", Oxford University Press, London.

Gosal, G.S. and Krishna, G. (1975), "Patterns of internal migration in India", in Kosinski, L.A. and Prothero, R.M. (eds.), 193-206.

Graves, T.D. (1966), "Alternative models for the study of urban migration", *Human Organisation,* 25, 295-99.

Gray, R. (1975), "Selections and allocation in council housing", *Transactions, Institute of British Geographers,* N.S.I., pp. 34-46.

Grigg, D.B. (1977), "E.G. Ravenstein and the 'Laws' of Migration", *Journal of Historical Geography,* 3, 41-54.

Ghabra Shaffeq (1991), "The Iraqi occupation of Kuwait - An eyewitness account", *Journal of Palestinian Studies,* 20, 112-125.

Ghai, D.S. and Ghai, P. (eds.) (1970), "Portraits of a Minority", Oxford University. Press, London.

Gilani, I. Jar, Khan, K.F. and Iqbal, M. (1981), "Labour migration from Pakistan to middle east and its impact on the domestic economy", *Research Report Series,* Islamabad.

Grigg, D.B. (1977), "E.G. Revenstein and the Laws of Migration", *Journal of Historical Geography,* 3, 41-54.

Gulati, Leela (1983), "Impacts of Male Migration to the Middle-East on the Family: some evidence from Kerala", *Economic and Political Weekly,* Bombay, No. 52, December 1983.

Haenszel, W. (1967), "Concert, measurement and data in migration analysis", Demography, 4, 253-62.

Hagerstrand, T. (1957), "Migration and area: survey of a sample of Swedish migration fields and hypothetical considerations of their genesis", in Hannerberg, D. *et al.* (1957), pp. 27-158.

Haggett, P. (1965), "Locational Analysis in Human Geography", Edward Arnold, London.

Harris, A.I. and Clausen, R. (1963), "Labour Mobility in Great Britain", 1953-63, HMSO, London.

Harris, J.R. and Todaro, M.P. (1970), "Migration, unemployment and development: a two sector analysis", *American Economic Review* 60, 126-42.

Harvey, D. (1973), "Social Justice and the City", Arnold, London.

Harvey, M.E. and Riddell, J.B. (1975), "Development, urbanization and migration : a test of a hypothesis in the third world", in Kosinski, L.A. and Protheroe, R.M. (eds.), pp. 51-66.

Henderson, J.R. (1978) 'Spatial re-organization: a geographic dimension in acculturation', *Canadian Geographer*, 22,1-21.

Herberle, R. (1938) 'The causes of the rural-urban migration: a survey of German theories', *American Journal of Sociology*, 43, 932-50.

Houston, C.J. (1978) 'Administrative control of migration to Moscow 1959-75', *Canadian Geographer*, 23, 32-44.

Hunter, A. (1974) 'Community change', *American Journal of Sociology*, 79, 923-47.

Hyman, G. and Gleave, D. (1978) "A reasonable theory of migration", *Transactions, Institute of British Geographers*, N.S. 3, 179-201.

Hagerstrand, T. (1957), "Migration and Area - Survey of a sample of swedish migration fields and hypothetical consideration of their genesis", in Hannesberg, pp. 27-158.

Imogene, S.O. (1967) 'Psycho-social factors in rural-urban migration', *Nigerian Journal of Economic and Social Studies*, 9, 375-85.

Jones, R.C. (1980) 'The role of perception in urban in-migration: a path analytic model', *Geographical Analysis,* 12, 98-108.

Jackson, J.A. (1969) (ed), "Migration, Sociological Studies 2", Cambridge University Press, Cambridge.

Jain, P.C. (1982), "Indians abroad: A current populations estimate", *Economic and Political Weekly,* 20-Feb, pp. 299-304.

Jansen, C.J. (1970), "Reading in the Sociology of Migration", Pargamon, Oxford.

Julian Wolpert (1970), "Behavioural aspects of decision to migrate", *in population geography A reader* - By G.J. Deko, McGraw Hill.

Kant, K. (1962) 'Classification and problems in migration', in Wanger, P.L. and Mikesell, M.W. (eds.) Readings in Cultural Geography, University of Chicago Press, Chicago, 47-57.

Keowan, P.A. (1971) 'The career cycle and the stepwise migration process', *New Zealand Geographer,* 27, 175-84.

Kirby, A.M. (1976) 'Housing market studies: a critical review', *Transactions,* Institute of British Geographiers, N.S.I., pp. 2-9.

Kabbra Abdurrahman Haitham Shoukat (1988), "Islamic Banluing : A case study of Kuwait", Ph.D. Thesis.

Keeley Charles (1980), "Asian workers migration to middle east", Working Paper No. 52, Centre for Policy Studies, The Population Council, New York.

Khalidi Walid (1991), "The Gulf crisies - Origin and Consequences", *Journal of Palestinian Studies,* 20, 5-28.

Kim, Suyoria (1982), "Contract migration in the republic of Korea", International Migration for Employment, Working Paper No. 4, ILO, Geneva, 1982.

Kondapi, L. (1951), *Indians Overseas (1838-1949),* Oxford University Press, Madras.

Kosinshi, L.A. and Protherto, R.M. (1975), *People in the Move, Studies in Internal Migration,* Metheun, London.

Kurup, B.S., "Determinants and consequences of migration", Sharif Bhownisk - *Economic and Political Weekly,* April 7, 1984, pp. 589-590.

Lee, E.S. (1966) 'A theory of migration', *Demography,* 3,47-57.

Lewis, W.C. (1977) 'The role of age in the decision to migrate', *Annals of Regional Science,* 11,51-60.

Lipset, S. and Bendix, R.(1952) 'Social mobility and occupational career paths', *American Journal of Sociology,* 57, 366-74.

Litwak, E. (1960) 'Geographic mobility and extended family cohesion', *American Sociological Review,* 25, 385-94.

Lowenthal, D. and Comitas, L. (1962) 'Emigration and depopulation: some neglected aspects of population geography', *Geographical Review,* 52, 195-210.

Lowry, I.S. (1966) *Migration and Metropolitan Growth: Two Analytical Models,* Chandler, San Francisco.

Leela Gulati, "Male Migration to middle East and the impact on the family - some evidence from Kerala", *Economic and Political Weekly,* Dec. 4-31, 1983, pp. 2217-25.

Lewis, G.J. (1974), "Human Migration", Unit 9, Regional Analysis and Development, Open University Press, Milton Keynes.

Looney, R.E. (1992), "Manpower option in a small labour importing state: The influence of ethnic composition in Kuwaits development", *International Migration,* 30-2 June, pp. 175-200.

Lowry, I.S. (1966), "Migration and Metropolitan Growth", *Two Analytical Models,* Candler, San Fransisco.

Mobogunje, A.K. (1970) 'A systems approach to a theory of rural-urban migration', *Geographical Analysis,* 2, 1-18.

Mangalam, J.J. (1968) *Human Migration,* University of Kentucky Press, Lexington, KY.

Meyer, R. (1980) 'A descriptive model of constrained residential search', *Geographical Analysis,* 12, 21-32.

Miller, S.J. (1970) 'Family life cycle: extended family orientations and economic aspirations as factors in the propensity to move', *Sociological Quarterly,* 17, 323-35.

Mitchell, G.D. (1950) 'Depopulation and rural social structure', *Sociological Review,* 42, 69-85.

Moorfe, E.G. (1971) 'Comments on the use of ecological models in the study of residential mobility in the city', *Economic Geography,* 47, 72-85.

Morgan, S.S. (1973) 'Why families move: a re-examination', *Professional Geographer,* 25, 124-9.

Morrison, P.A. (1967) 'Duration of residence and prospective migration: the evaluation of a stochastic model', Demography, 4, 553-61.

Musgrave, F. (1963) The Migratory Elite, Heinemann, London.

Madhevan, M.C. (1985), "Indian Emigrants, Numbers, Characteristics, and Economic Impact", *Population and Development Review,* Vol. 11, No. 3, September 1985, pp. 457-481.

Manolo, I. Abella (1984), "Labour migration from South and South East Asia: Some policy issues", *International Labour Review,* Vol. 123, No. 4, July-August, 1984.

Mathew, E.T, Gopinath Nair, "Socio-Economic characteristics of Emigrants and Emigrants households - A case study of two villages in Kerala", *Economic and Political Weekly,* pp. 1141-53.

Mathew, S.J. (1983), "Letter from Kerala", *For Eastern Economic Review,* January 27, 1983.

Maylah Mohammad Hassan (1987), "The International labour migration to Kuwait, its impacts, determinants and future prospects", Ph.D. Thesis.

Mongalam, J.J. (1968), "Human Migration", University of Kenturkey, Press.

Mowad Galal Abdulla (1987), "Urbanisation and labour migration in the Arab countries of the Gulf", *Journal of the Gulf and Arabrian* Penisula Studies, 1987, 13, 31, July.

Nagi-Mustafa, H. (1988), "Consequences of International Migration for Work to the Oil rich countries in the middle east - A political economy perspective".

Nair, P.R., Gopinathan (1983), "Asian emigration to the middle east: Emigration from India", *Trivandrum Centre for Development Studies,* Working Paper No. 180.

Nanjundan, S. (1950), "Indians in Malayan Economy", Office of Registrar, Government of India, New Delhi.

Omvedt, G. (1980), "Migration in colonial India: The articulation of feudalism and capitalism by the colonial state", *The Journal of Peasant Studies,* 6, No. 2.

Oomen T.K. (1989), "India - Brain drain of the migration of Talent", *International Migration,* 27, 3 September, pp. 411-25.

Parkes, D.N. and Thrift, N.J. (1980) *Times, Spaces and Places,* Wiley, London.

Patten, J. (1976) 'Patterns of migration and movement of labour to three pre-industrial East Anglian towns', *Journal of Historical Geography,* 2, 111-29.

Partha S Ghosh, "Our Gulf policy - some nagging doubts", *Mainstream,* Sept. 8, 1990, p.11.

Prakash B.A., "Impact of Foreign remittances - A case study of chavakkad village in Kerala", *Economic and Political Weekly,* pp. 1106-11.

Prayer, R.J. (1979), *"Internal Migration and Urbanisation".*

Ravenstgein, E.G. (1885;18889) 'The laws of migration', *Journal of the Royal Statistical Society,* 48 (1885), 167-235; and 52 (1889). 241-305.

Rees, G. and Rees, T. (1977) 'Alternatives to the census: the example of sources of internal migration data', *Town Planning Review,* 48, 123-40.

Rex, J.A. and Moore, R. (1967) *Race, Community and Conflict,* Oxford University Press, London.

Richmond, A.H. (1968) 'Return migration of Britons from Canada', *Population Studies,* 22, 263-71.

Rose, A.M. (1958) 'Distance of migration and the socio-economic status of migrants', *American Sociological Review,* 23, 420-3.

Roseman, C.C. (1971) 'Migration as a spatial and temporal process', *Annals, Association of American Geographers,* 61, 589-98.

Rashid Amjad (1987), "To the Gulf and Bach", Studies on the economic impact on Asian Labour migration - ILO (ARATEP - Asian Regional Team for Employment Promotion), edited, New Delhi.

Ratna Naidu (1987), "Old cities and New predicaments".

Rizwanul Islam (1980), "Export of manpower from Bangla Desh to Middle east countries - The impact of remittance money on household expenditure", NFRHRD, Dhaka.

Schneider, C.H.P. (1975) 'Models of space searching in urban areas', *Geographical Analysis,* 7, 173-86.

Shaw, R.P. (1974) 'A note on cost-relative calculations and decisions to migrate', *Population Studies,* 28, 167-9.

Stewart, C.T. (1960) 'Migration as a function of population and distance', *American Sociological Review,* 25, 347-56.

Stouffer, S.A. (1940) 'Intervening opportunities: a theory relating mobility and distance', *American Sociological Review,* 5, 845-67.

Stub, H.R. (1962) 'The occupational characteristics of migrants to Duluth: a retest of Rose's hypothesis' *American Sociological* Review, 27, 87-90.

Savart, L.M. (1976) 'Environmental preference migration: a review', *Geographical Review,* 66, 314-30.

Sandhu, K.S. (1969), "Indians in Malaya: Some aspects of their immigration and settlement", 1786-1957, London, Cambridge University Press.

Sen-Kasturi (1986), "Migrants from Indian sub-continent and the Kuwait labour market - Economic, Political and Social Determinants", Ph.D Thesis.

Shah Nasra, M.Al-Qudsi-Sulayaman S, and Shajkh Maqdoom. A. (1991), "Asian women workers in Kuwait", *International Migration Review,* 25.

Shaheed, Farida (1981), "Migration and effects on women in the villages", *Seminar - Rural development of women,* Mahabaleshwar, India.

Sharma, P.C. (1978), "Population Migration", *A Selected Bibliographical research guide* 1972-77, Public Administration Series.

Show, R.P. (1975), "Migration theory and Fact", *A Review and Bibliography of current literature.*

Show, R.P. (1975). *op cit.*

Siddiqui, A.M.A.H (1983), "Economic and Non-economic impact of migration from Bangla Desh — An Overview", Dhaka Manpower Planning Centre.

Simmie, J.M. (1972), *The Sociology of Information Migration,* Centre for Environmental studies, London.

Sirajeldin (1983), "I and others, Manpower and international migration in the middle east and north Africa", *A World Bank Publication,* Oxford University Press.

Soman H. Chowdhry (1986), "Labour migration to the middle east: An Asian perspective", *Asian Economic Review,* April 1986, pp. 43-73.

Spencer, R.F. (1970), "Migration and Anthropology", University of Washington Press, Seattle.

Stabl, Charles, W. (1981), "Contract labour migration from Philippines, Trends and Issues", *Conference on Internatgional Migration in the Arab World,* May 11-16, Nicosia, Cyprus.

Thomas, B. (1954) *Migration and Economic Growth,* Cambridge University Press, Cambridge.

Tadaro, M.P. (1969), 'A model of labour migration and urban unemployment in less developed countries', *American Economic Review,* 59, 138-48.

Tan, Edita (1987), "Migration savings, remittances and labour supply behaviour - a comperative experience of Asian countries", ILO (ARTEP), New Delhi.

Thomos, D.S. (1954), "Population re-distribution and economic growth", U.S. - American Philosophical Society.

Tinker, H. (1977), "The Banyal Tree: The overseas Immigrants from India, Pakistan and Bangla Desh", Oxford, Oxford University Press.

Todaro, M.P. (1969), "A model of labour migration and urban unemployment in less developmed countries", *American Economic Review,* 59, 138-48.

Turner, J. (1976), "Housing by people", Marion Boyars, London.

Webber, M.J., Symanski. R. and Root, J. (1975) 'Toward a Cognitive Spatial Theory', *Economic Geography,* 51, 100-16.

Weinberg, A.A. (1961), *"Migration and Belonging: a Study of Mental Health and Personal Adjustment* in Israel", Martinus Nijhoff, The Hague.

Wolpert, J. (1964), 'The decision process in spatial perspective', *Annals, Association of American Geographers,* 54, 220-9.

Woods, R. (1979), *Population in Geography,* Longman, London.

Weiner, Myrun (1982), "International and Development: Indians in the Persian Gulf", *Population and Development Review,* March 1982.

Willis, K.G. (1974), *Problems in Migration Analysis,* Saxon House, Farnborough.

Word, R.J. (1980), "Migration, Myth and Magic in Papua New Guinea, Australian", *Geographical Studies,* 18, 119-34.

Zachariah, K.C. (1964), *An Historical Study of Internal Migration in the Indian Sub-continent 1901-31,* Asia Publishing House, Bombay.

Zelinsky, W. (1962), 'Changes in the geographic patterns of rural population in the United States 1790-1960', *Geographical Review,* 52, 492-524.

Zelinshy, W. (1971), "The hypothesis of the mobility transition:, *Geographical Review,* 61, 219-49.

